READERS' FAVOURITE RECIPES

Dear Readers

An interest in cookery sparks off a response in many people, and when we launched a series of national competitions, the entries came in by the thousand. In each contest 72 semi-finalists from all over the country cooked their original recipes before an invited audience. Of these, only 12 finalists were chosen, who went on to compete for the prizes.

We felt that these recipes were too good to keep to ourselves, so we have published them for you in this book. Our regular *Family Circle* readers generously share their favourite recipes with our Cookery Department, who lose no time in trying them out; Reader Club members, too, have made their contribution to our recipe files. Some of the very best of these are included here; and a large number have been photographed to illustrate one of the important aspects of a good recipe – that it looks delectable, too. The recipes form a collection for meals for every occasion. You'll entertain confidently with the delicious dinner party dishes, while, for less formal occasions, you can choose from the buffet meals chapter. There's a dazzling array of gorgeous desserts: cheesecakes, trifles, gâteaux – just making these satisfies the creative instinct in us.

Among our main meal selections you'll find a great many cost-conscious dishes. We've included them because they are quick to make and have withstood the kind of popularity tests that only hungry families can provide! And, for those busy days in the middle of the week, there are plenty of snack meals and home-from-school high teas. They have been developed by ingenious mums who know what children like as well as appreciating what's good for them.

Also, to make you one of the most enviable mums around, we've picked out some attractive, unusual novelty cakes – like a fire engine, a dog, an owl – which will delight a birthday boy or girl.

Let us just add that, if this book should inspire you to create more new dishes of your own, do keep sending them to us at *Family Circle*, so that we can start putting them together for Volume Two. Good cooking!

Family Circle Editor

CONTENTS

ELM TREE BOOKS

METRICATION

The recipes in this book were all sent to us with ingredients given in imperial amounts: pounds, ounces and pints. As many people are now using metric recipes, and schoolchildren are learning this method exclusively, we have converted all the recipes to use both metric as well as imperial amounts.

They have all been tested in the Family Circle kitchen to make sure that a good result can be obtained whichever system is used. The amounts are not exactly equal, so it is important to use either one system or the other throughout. To help you to convert your own imperial recipes when using metric equipment, here is how it is done.

Weighing
The exact conversion of 1oz to 28.349 grams makes an exact calculation impossible. To make it easier, the Metrication Board has suggested that 1oz is taken as 25 grams (abbreviated as g), when working with amounts below 1lb, and 1oz to be 30g, when working above 1lb.

The large metric amount is called a kilogram (1,000g) abbreviated to kg. It is equivalent to 2.2lb. Many familiar foods are already packed in this amount; sugar was one of the first to change. To keep the proportion right, 1lb is converted to ½kg.

The following chart of equivalents should help you obtain the correct proportion of ingredients when you cook.

For amounts up to 1lb:
    25g = 1oz
    50g = 2oz
    75g = 3oz
    100g = 4oz
    200g = 8oz
    400g = 1lb

For amounts over 1lb:
    30g = 1oz
    60g = 2oz
    125g = 4oz
    ¼kg (250g) = 8oz
    ½kg (500g) = 1lb
    1kg (1,000g) = 2lb

Liquids
The metric measurement for liquids is a litre. Fractions are called millilitres, abbreviated to ml.

A pint is equivalent to 0.568 litres, a difficult amount to calculate, so this amount has been rounded down to 0.500 litres or 500 millilitres. This is the same proportion as for the gram measurement, both being about 10 per cent less than their imperial equivalents and the recipes converted this way work well.

The conversion chart is as follows:
    1 litre (1,000ml) = 2 pints
    ½ litre (500ml) = 1 pint
    250ml = ½ pint
    125ml = ¼ pint

Spoon measurements
It is always the smallest amounts that are the most difficult to measure, yet it is often these ingredients which are the most important to get right. It is essential, for instance, to add the correct amount of liquid flavouring or spice to a dish and it is even more important to measure the correct amount of raising agent such as baking powder or bicarbonate of soda.

Using the first teaspoon that comes to hand in the cutlery drawer, is a rather 'hit and miss' way of measuring. All teaspoons are different and one day your cake will be well risen, the next day it will be a disaster. The same applies to tablespoons; Granny's huge Victorian-style spoons hold about twice as much as the modern Scandinavian-styled tablespoons that are generally used nowadays. It becomes difficult to repeat the success of a particular recipe, especially if awkward ingredients like golden syrup have to be measured.

Metric measuring spoons are a worthwhile buy if you want to avoid such problems. These spoons are calibrated by volume in millilitres, which may seem odd for measuring solid ingredients, but it works well and they are easy to use. You should always level the ingredients in the spoons, easily done by using the back of a knife.

The spoon measurements convert as follows:
    15ml spoon = 1 level tablespoon
    10ml spoon = 1 level dessertspoon or 1 rounded teaspoon
    5ml spoon = 1 level teaspoon
    2.5ml spoon = ½ level teaspoon

Working in metric is very easy, but please remember to use either the metric or the imperial amounts exclusively.

CAKES AND COOKIES

*We're always very
impressed by our readers'
patience and inventiveness when it comes to making cakes and
cookies. Here are some of their recipes to delight the children*

Windmill Cake

(pictured on page 8)

*Mrs Margaret Jones, from Canterbury in Kent, made this
cake for her daughter's fourth birthday.*

METRIC	IMPERIAL
CAKE	CAKE
150g soft margarine	**6oz soft margarine**
150g castor sugar	**6oz castor sugar**
150g self-raising flour	**6oz self-raising flour**
50g cornflour	**1½oz cornflour**
3 × 2.5ml spoons baking powder	**1½ level teaspoons baking powder**
3 eggs	**3 eggs**
Apricot jam	**Apricot jam**
SATIN ICING	SATIN ICING
50g margarine	**1½oz margarine**
2 × 10ml spoons lemon juice	**1½ tablespoons lemon juice**
About ½kg icing sugar	**About 1lb 4oz icing sugar**
Pink, brown, yellow, purple and red food colourings	**Pink, brown, yellow, purple and red food colourings**
Cornflour	**Cornflour**
DECORATION	DECORATION
25g desiccated coconut	**1oz desiccated coconut**
Green food colouring	**Green food colouring**
1 (20cm) round silver cake board	**1 (8in) round silver cake board**
Birthday cake candles	**Birthday cake candles**
3 ice cream wafers	**3 ice cream wafers**

1. To make cake: prepare a cool oven (170 deg C, 325 deg F, Gas Mark 3). Brush a ¾ litre (1½ pint), a ½ litre (¾ pint) and a 125ml (¼ pint) ovenglass pudding basin with melted fat. Line bases with greaseproof paper; grease paper. Place basins on a baking sheet.

2. Place margarine, castor sugar, flour, cornflour, baking powder and eggs in a bowl. Mix with a wooden spoon; beat for 1 to 2 minutes, until smooth and glossy.

3. Half fill each basin with mixture; level tops with back of a metal spoon. Bake in centre of oven for 20 to 30 minutes for a 125ml (¼ pint) size, 30 to 40 minutes for a ½ litre (¾ pint) size and 50 to 60 minutes for a ¾ litre (1½ pint) size.

4. Test by pressing cakes with the fingers. If cooked, cakes should spring back and have begun to shrink from sides of basins. Leave to cool in basins for 5 to 10 minutes. Loosen edges with a knife, turn out cakes, remove paper; leave to cool completely on a wire rack.

5. Place apricot jam in a small saucepan, heat gently until melted; remove from heat. Sieve jam into a basin.

6. To make satin icing: heat margarine, lemon juice and 2 × 10ml spoons (1½ tablespoons) water in a medium saucepan until margarine has melted. Sift icing sugar. Add 150g (6oz) icing sugar and stir over a low heat until sugar has dissolved; heat for 2 minutes, when mixture should begin to boil gently. (Do not boil syrup quickly, or icing will be too hard to work.) Remove from heat and add 150g (6oz) icing sugar. Beat with a wooden spoon, then pour into a bowl and beat well, scraping mixture down from side of bowl. Gradually add sufficient icing sugar to make the consistency of soft dough. Turn out on to a board dusted with icing sugar; knead until smooth and white. Place in a well sealed polythene bag until required.

7. Cut off a quarter of icing; return to polythene bag. Colour remainder pink; place in a polythene bag.

8. Place coconut in a basin; add a few drops of green colouring; mix together until evenly coloured. Brush cake board with apricot jam; sprinkle with coconut.

9. Brush tops and sides of each cake with jam; stack cakes on top of each other, largest at the bottom.

10. Sprinkle a board with cornflour; roll out pink icing to an oblong, 43cm (17in) by 20cm (8in). Along top edge of icing, measure 11.5cm (4½in) at each side and cut diagonally from these marks to base corner (see diagram). Top edge should measure 20cm (8in) and base 43cm (17in).

11. Wrap icing around cake; trim and smooth join with well cornfloured fingers. Place on cake board.

12. Knead icing trimmings together; cut in half. Roll 1 piece into a ball and place on top of cake; shape into a dome. Cut one third off other piece of pink icing and roll into a ball; reserve for securing the sails.

13. To make candle holders: dip fingers in cornflour, take a small piece of pink icing and press out to a circle with the fingers. Pinch at one side, to form a petal shape. Curl petal inwards, forming centre of flower. Press out another 2 pieces of icing, to make 2 more petals and wrap around centre petal, to form a small flower. Cut off stalk, place candle in centre and leave to set on a plate. Make enough candle holders for the child's age.

14. To make sails: cut 2 wafers in half diagonally; brush edges of wafers with a little apricot jam. Cut reserved icing into 4 pieces. Colour 1 piece brown with food colouring; cut off two thirds and roll out 4, 23cm (9in) lengths between the hands. Stick around edge of sails. Roll out 1, 26.5cm (10½in) length and cut into strips to fit sails (see picture on page 8). Using a little jam, secure 1 of each length of icing on sails, to form slats.

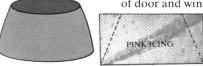

15. Cut remaining wafer in half widthwise and cut 1 piece in half again. Shape the top of largest piece of wafer into a door and the smaller pieces into 2 windows. Using remaining brown icing, roll into thin lengths and secure around edge of door and windows with jam.

PINK ICING

16. Fix door and windows on to front of windmill with a little jam. On the back of each sail, stick a small strip of icing and stick sails in position with a little jam. Place reserved ball of pink icing on to centre of sails, to secure.
17. Colour remaining icing yellow, purple and red.
18. To make flowers: dip fingers in cornflour, take a small piece of coloured icing and press out to a circle. Pinch at one side, to form a petal shape; curl petal inwards. Make 2 more curled petals and press them together. Cut off the stalk of each and leave flowers to dry on a plate.
19. Arrange candles and flowers around cake board.

Brown Owl Cake

(pictured on page 9)

Mrs Eileen Bass, from Hackney in East London, made this cake for her daughter Andrea's Brownie club party.

METRIC	IMPERIAL
CAKE	CAKE
250g soft margarine	**10oz soft margarine**
250g castor sugar	**10oz castor sugar**
5 eggs	**5 eggs**
250g self-raising flour	**10oz self-raising flour**
75g cornflour	**2½oz cornflour**
5 × 2.5ml spoons baking powder	**2½ level teaspoons baking powder**
1 × 2.5ml spoon vanilla essence	**½ teaspoon vanilla essence**
50g desiccated coconut	**2oz desiccated coconut**
Green food colouring	**Green food colouring**

1(23cm) round silver cake board	**1 (9in) round silver cake board**
2 × 15ml spoons golden syrup	**1 rounded tablespoon golden syrup**

COFFEE BUTTER ICING	COFFEE BUTTER ICING
1 × 15ml spoon instant coffee	**1 level tablespoon instant coffee**
2 × 15ml spoons boiling water	**2 tablespoons boiling water**
300g icing sugar	**12oz icing sugar**
150g butter	**6oz butter**

DECORATION	DECORATION
2 brown-coloured chocolate beans	**2 brown-coloured chocolate beans**
Half a large Brazil nut	**Half a large Brazil nut**
7 large chocolate flake bars	**7 large chocolate flake bars**

1. Prepare a cool oven (170 deg C, 325 deg F, Gas Mark 3).
2. Brush 2, ¾ litre (1½ pint) ovenglass pudding basins with melted fat. Line bases with greaseproof paper; grease paper.
3. To make cake: place margarine, castor sugar, eggs, flour, cornflour, baking powder and vanilla essence in a bowl; mix with a wooden spoon. Beat for 1 to 2 minutes, until the mixture is smooth and glossy.
4. Divide mixture equally between basins; level tops with back of a metal spoon. Bake cakes in centre of oven for 1 hour 5 minutes to 1½ hours. Test by pressing with the fingers. If cooked, cakes should spring back and have begun to shrink from sides of basins. Leave to cool in basins for 5 to 10 minutes. Loosen edges with a round-ended knife, turn out, remove paper; leave cakes to cool completely on a wire rack.
5. Place coconut in a small basin, add a few drops of green food colouring and mix until evenly coloured. Brush cake board with warmed golden syrup and sprinkle with green coconut, to represent grass.
6. To make coffee icing: blend coffee and boiling water together in a basin. Sift icing sugar into a bowl; add butter and coffee. Beat together until light and fluffy.
7. Split each cake in half horizontally; sandwich halves together with a little icing. Trim tops of each cake to level, if necessary. Spread flat side of one cake with icing and sandwich cakes together, to form a large, oval cake. Place cake on board and spread with remaining icing to cover, making icing thicker at each side of head.
8. Using a small palette knife, shape an ear with icing each side of head (see picture on page 9).
9. Using a pointed knife, mark 2, 4cm (1½in) rings on top of owl, for eyes. In centre of each, place a chocolate bean. Below eyes, mark an oval, 9cm (3½in) across, to represent downy front (see picture). Place half a large Brazil nut in position, for beak (see picture).
10. Using a sharp knife, cut chocolate flake bars into sticks. Press into the coffee butter icing, to cover the owl completely except for features and downy front.

7

WINDMILL CAKE *Recipe on page 6*

BROWN OWL CAKE *Recipe on page 7* ▶

Candy Cottage Cake

(pictured on page 12)

Mrs Cutcliffe, from Crowthorne in Berkshire, made this cake for her daughter's fourth birthday.

METRIC	IMPERIAL
CAKE	CAKE
150g soft margarine	**6oz soft margarine**
150g castor sugar	**6oz castor sugar**
3 eggs	**3 eggs**
150g self-raising flour	**6oz self-raising flour**
50g cocoa	**1½oz cocoa**
3 × 2.5ml spoons baking powder	**1½ level teaspoons baking powder**
50g desiccated coconut	**2oz desiccated coconut**
Green food colouring	**Green food colouring**
1 (25cm) square silver cake board	**1 (10in) square silver cake board**
1 × 15ml spoon golden syrup	**1 level tablespoon golden syrup**
BUTTER ICING	BUTTER ICING
300g icing sugar	**12oz icing sugar**
150g butter	**6oz butter**
2 × 15ml spoons cocoa	**2 level tablespoons cocoa**
2 × 15ml spoons boiling water	**2 tablespoons boiling water**
DECORATION	DECORATION
50g chocolate-flavoured sugar strands	**2oz chocolate-flavoured sugar strands**
2 (256g) boxes liquorice allsorts	**2 (9oz) boxes liquorice allsorts**
4 mushroom candle holders	**4 mushroom candle holders**
4 yellow candles	**4 yellow candles**

1. Prepare a cool oven (170 deg C, 325 deg F, Gas Mark 3). Brush a deep, 18cm (7in) square tin with melted fat. Line base of tin with greaseproof paper; grease paper.

2. Place margarine, castor sugar and eggs in a bowl. Sift flour, 50g (1½oz) cocoa and baking powder into bowl. Mix together with a wooden spoon; beat for 1 to 2 minutes, until mixture is smooth and glossy.

3. Spread mixture in tin; level top with back of a metal spoon. Bake in centre of oven for 50 to 65 minutes. Test by pressing with the fingers. If cooked, cake should spring back and have begun to shrink from sides of tin.

4. Leave to cool in tin for 5 to 10 minutes. Loosen edges with a round-ended knife, turn out, remove paper and leave to cool completely on a wire rack.

5. Place coconut in a small basin; add a few drops of green food colouring and mix together until evenly coloured. Brush cake board with warmed syrup and sprinkle with coconut.

6. To make icing: sift icing sugar into a bowl. Add butter; beat together until light and fluffy. Blend together 2 × 15ml spoons (2 level tablespoons) cocoa and boiling water in a basin; leave to cool. Mix thoroughly into butter icing.

7. Cut cake in half to make 2 oblongs. Cut one oblong in half to make 2 squares and each square in half to make 4 triangles (see diagram 1). With a little chocolate butter icing, sandwich triangles of cake together, to form a roof. Spread sides of other cake with butter icing. Place chocolate sugar strands on a piece of greaseproof paper. Coat long sides of cake with chocolate strands. Place base on board and spread some butter icing over top of cake. Place roof on top of cake and cover roof and ends of house with butter icing (see diagram 2).

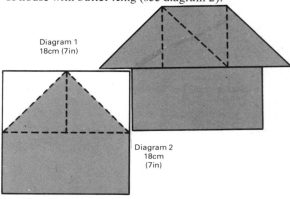

Diagram 1
18cm (7in)

Diagram 2
18cm (7in)

8. To decorate house: sort liquorice sweets into varieties. Cut 2 triangles from side of roof and press in 2 yellow, black and white layer sweets for chimney surrounds. Place a little icing on base of plain liquorice tubes and place in centre of each, as chimney pots.

9. Place 1 plain liquorice tube at each end of top of roof, for roof posts. Cut 6 yellow, black and white layer sweets in halves, to form triangles, and place, cut sides downwards, on top of roof.

10. Cut 8 orange, 8 pink and 8 brown layer sweets in halves, through liquorice centres. Starting from bottom edge of roof, place a row each of brown, white, pink, white and orange sweets, overlapping, on both sides of roof, to represent tiles.

11. Cut each of 6 white-centre liquorice tubes in 4 slices and place, side by side, on front and back of house to represent gables. Cut 4 beaded liquorice sweets in halves and place down front and back corners of house.

12. Place 1 pink beaded sweet on each end of house, to represent windows. Cut 2 plain liquorice tubes in halves lengthwise; arrange at front end of house, to represent door. Cut 1 blue beaded sweet into quarters. Place one quarter on top of door and cut another quarter sweet in half and place 1 on door, to represent handle. Cut round yellow sweets with liquorice centres in halves, to make thin rounds. Cut each piece in half again, to make half circles. Place a little icing on base of each sweet and arrange around edge of board, to form a fence. Snip a small 'U' out of each of remaining beaded sweets, to represent flowers. Arrange on grass and place a small piece of cut-out liquorice sweet on top. Place mushroom candle holders on board and place a candle in each.

Patch the Dog

(pictured on page 12)

Miss Cheryl Pearce, from Cheam in Surrey, sent us her clever idea for Patch the Dog.

METRIC	IMPERIAL
CAKE	CAKE
150g soft margarine	**6oz soft margarine**
150g castor sugar	**6oz castor sugar**
3 eggs	**3 eggs**
150g self-raising flour	**6oz self-raising flour**
3 × 2.5ml spoons baking powder	**1½ level teaspoons baking powder**
1 × 5ml spoon vanilla essence	**1 teaspoon vanilla essence**
25g desiccated coconut	**1oz desiccated coconut**
Red food colouring	**Red food colouring**
1 (25cm) square silver cake board	**1 (10in) square silver cake board**
Apricot jam	**Apricot jam**
ICING	ICING
500g icing sugar	**1lb icing sugar**
250g butter	**8oz butter**
1 × 15ml spoon cocoa	**3 level teaspoons cocoa**
Boiling water	**Boiling water**
1 × 5ml spoon instant coffee	**1 level teaspoon instant coffee**
Green food colouring	**Green food colouring**

1. Prepare a moderate oven (170 deg C, 325 deg F, Gas Mark 3). Brush a 25cm (10in) square tin with melted fat. Line base of tin with greaseproof paper; grease paper.
2. Place margarine, sugar, eggs, flour, baking powder and vanilla essence in a bowl; beat for 1 to 2 minutes. Spread mixture in tin.
3. Bake in centre of oven for 40 to 50 minutes. Test by pressing with the fingers. If cooked, cake should spring back and have begun to shrink from sides of tin. Cool for 5 to 10 minutes; loosen edges with a round-ended knife, turn out, remove paper and leave to cool on a wire rack.
4. Place coconut in a small basin, add a few drops red food colouring; mix until evenly coloured pink. Brush cake board with a little warmed apricot jam and sprinkle with coconut.
5. Sift icing sugar into a bowl. Add butter and beat together until light and fluffy. Place 2 × 15ml spoons (1 rounded tablespoon) icing in a small basin and reserve.
6. Divide remaining butter icing between 2 basins. Dissolve cocoa in 1 × 15ml spoon (3 teaspoons) boiling water; dissolve instant coffee in 1 × 10ml spoon (2 teaspoons) boiling water. Leave both to cool.
7. Beat cocoa into butter icing in one basin and coffee into the other.
8. Using diagram as a guide, draw and cut out shape in greaseproof paper. (Note: baked cake will measure 22.5cm (9in) square.)
9. Place paper shape on cake and secure with a couple of pins. Carefully, using a sharp knife, cut around paper pattern. Remove excess cake (this can be used to make a trifle).
10. Using the point of the knife, mark small guidelines through paper on to cake to make the features. Remove pins and paper; place dog on cake board.
11. Place 2 × 15ml spoons (1 rounded tablespoon) chocolate icing in a greaseproof paper piping bag, fitted with a plain writing tube. Pipe feature lines on top of cake.
12. Place remaining chocolate icing in a greaseproof paper piping bag, fitted with a small star tube. Pipe stars on unshaded areas, excluding eyes, on top and sides of cake (see diagram).
13. Place coffee icing in a greaseproof paper piping bag, fitted with star tube. Pipe stars in shaded areas (see diagram).
14. Re-pipe main feature lines, using plain tube and chocolate icing. Pipe a curved line on each ear, 3 lines on 2 coffee-iced paws and 2 lines on front paw. Pipe beads of icing in centre of each eye.
15. Divide reserved butter icing into 3 portions. Add a few drops of green colouring to one third of the icing and a few drops of red colouring to another third; beat until evenly coloured.
16. Place green icing in a greaseproof paper piping bag, fitted with plain writing tube. Pipe two rows of beads along collar of dog and pipe beads in medallion.
17. Place plain butter icing in a greaseproof paper piping bag, fitted with plain writing tube. Pipe beads around dog's eyes.
18. Place pink butter icing in a greaseproof paper piping bag, fitted with plain writing tube. Pipe beads between plain and chocolate icing on eyes. Pipe a mouth and the outline of a tongue on snout.
Note: a greaseproof piping bag with the end snipped to make a small hole can be used instead of a writing tube.

1 square represents 2.5cm (1in)

Coffee icing.

CANDY COTTAGE CAKE *Recipe on page 10*

PATCH THE DOG
Recipe on page 11 ▶

12

SPEED CAR CAKE *Recipe on page 14*

Speed Car Cake

(pictured on page 13)

Miss Joy Chittenden, from Felbridge in West Sussex, supplied this idea for a little boy's birthday cake.

METRIC
CAKE
1 medium-sized orange
100g soft margarine
100g castor sugar
100g self-raising flour
1 × 5ml spoon baking
    powder
2 eggs

ICING
200g icing sugar
100g soft margarine
Orange food colouring

DECORATION
50g desiccated coconut
Green food colouring
1 (25cm) square silver
    cake board
1 × 15ml spoon golden
    syrup
5 gingernut biscuits
1 (256g) packet liquorice
    allsorts
1 × 15ml spoon cocoa
1 × 15ml spoon boiling
    water
2 round orange lollipops
Birthday cake candles and
    holders

IMPERIAL
CAKE
1 medium-sized orange
4oz soft margarine
4oz castor sugar
4oz self-raising flour
1 level teaspoon baking
    powder
2 eggs

ICING
8oz icing sugar
4oz soft margarine
Orange food colouring

DECORATION
1½oz desiccated coconut
Green food colouring
1 (10in) square silver cake
    board
1 level tablespoon golden
    syrup
5 gingernut biscuits
1 (9oz) packet liquorice
    allsorts
1 level tablespoon cocoa
1 tablespoon boiling
    water
2 round orange lollipops
Birthday cake candles and
    holders

1. To make cake: prepare a cool oven (170 deg C, 325 deg F, Gas Mark 3). Brush a round, 20cm (8in) sandwich tin with melted fat or oil. Line base with greaseproof paper; grease paper.

2. Scrub orange; grate rind finely. Squeeze juice; reserve for icing. Place 100g (4oz) margarine, sugar, flour, baking powder, eggs and rind in a bowl. Mix together with a wooden spoon; beat for 2 minutes, until mixture is smooth and glossy.

3. Place mixture in tin; level top with back of a metal spoon. Bake in centre of oven for 35 to 45 minutes. Test by pressing with the fingers. If cooked, cake should spring back and have begun to shrink from side of tin. Leave to cool in tin for 5 to 10 minutes, then turn out, remove paper and leave cake to cool completely on a wire rack.

4. To make icing: sift icing sugar into a bowl. Add 100g (4oz) margarine and about 1×15ml spoon (1 tablespoon) orange juice; beat until smooth. Beat in a few drops of orange food colouring.

5. Prepare a moderate grill. Remove rack from grill pan and sprinkle half the coconut into grill pan. Toast until coconut is golden brown; leave to cool. Place remaining

coconut in a small basin, add a few drops of green food colouring and mix until evenly coloured.

6. Brush cake board with warmed golden syrup. Sprinkle a 4cm (1½in) border of green coconut down 2 opposite sides of cake board, to represent grass. Fill in centre with toasted coconut, to represent the road.

7. Cut cake in half, to form 2 semi-circles (see diagram below left). Spread both halves with icing and sandwich together, to form one large semi-circle.

8. Cut out 2 triangles from rounded edge of cake, about 5cm (2in) from centre on each side of cake (see diagram below right), to shape car.

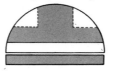 

9. Reserve 1 × 15ml spoon (1 tablespoon) of icing for decoration. Cover cake with remaining icing; spread evenly with a palette knife, shaping car smoothly.

10. Cut each triangle of cake in 2. Arrange on road on cake board as supports for car. Place car on supports near back edge of board.

11. Spread base of each biscuit with a little icing; press in position at front and back of car, to represent wheels. Place spare wheel on top of boot.

12. Cut 3 round yellow sweets with liquorice centres in halves, to form 6 thin rounds; spread a little icing on 5 rounds and stick on to wheels, to form hubs.

13. Cut 2 round pink sweets in halves, to form 4 lights. Press 2 on to front and 2 on to back of car.

14. Cut one yellow, black and white layer sweet into 3; place in position, in a line, with layers showing, to represent radiator grille.

15. Peel liquorice off 2 rolls, reserving white centres. Cut each piece of the liquorice into 2 strips; place around each corner of car, to represent bumpers.

16. Cut a small oblong out of each of 2 pink and white layered sweets. Place remaining L-shaped pieces of sweet in position on bonnet, to form wing mirrors.

17. Blend cocoa and water together; leave to cool. Add to reserved icing and beat until evenly coloured. Make a greaseproof paper piping bag; fill with chocolate icing. Snip end off bag.

18. Using 2 white square sweets, pipe the number of the child's age on to both sweets. Place at front and back of car, to represent number plates. Pipe doors and windows on to car with chocolate icing. Cut out liquorice door handles and place in position.

19. Make a pedestrian crossing in front of car across road, using brown and white layered sweets.

20. Thread on to each lollipop stick a black liquorice roll, a reserved white roll and another black roll, to represent Belisha beacons. Pierce 2 holes in cake board with a skewer, on each side of pedestrian crossing; place beacons in position.

21. Arrange birthday cake candles, in holders, in position on board.

Football Cake

(pictured on page 16)

Mrs Sheila Eade, who comes from Colchester, Essex, says her son was delighted with this birthday cake.

METRIC	IMPERIAL
CAKE	CAKE
150g soft margarine	**6oz soft margarine**
150g castor sugar	**6oz castor sugar**
3 eggs	**3 eggs**
150g self-raising flour	**6oz self-raising flour**
50g cornflour	**1½oz cornflour**
3 × 2.5ml spoons baking powder	**1½ level teaspoons baking powder**
1 × 2.5ml spoon vanilla essence	**½ teaspoon vanilla essence**
25g desiccated coconut	**1oz desiccated coconut**
Green food colouring	**Green food colouring**
2 × 15ml spoons golden syrup	**1 rounded tablespoon golden syrup**
1 (23cm) round silver cake board	**1 (9in) round silver cake board**
CHOCOLATE BUTTER ICING	CHOCOLATE BUTTER ICING
2 × 15ml spoons cocoa	**2 level tablespoons cocoa**
2 × 15ml spoons boiling water	**2 tablespoons boiling water**
200g icing sugar	**8oz icing sugar**
100g butter	**4oz butter**
SATIN ICING	SATIN ICING
50g margarine	**1½oz margarine**
2 × 10ml spoons lemon juice	**1½ tablespoons lemon juice**
About ½kg icing sugar	**About 1lb 4oz icing sugar**
Cornflour	**Cornflour**
DECORATION	DECORATION
6 green candles	**6 green candles**

1. To make cake: prepare a cool oven (170 deg C, 325 deg F, Gas Mark 3).

2. Brush 2, ¾ litre (1½ pint) ovenglass pudding basins with melted fat. Line bases with greaseproof paper; grease paper.

3. Place 150g (6oz) margarine, castor sugar, eggs, flour, cornflour, baking powder and vanilla essence in a bowl; mix together with a wooden spoon and beat for 1 to 2 minutes, until mixture is smooth and glossy.

4. Divide mixture equally between basins; level tops with back of metal spoon. Bake cakes in centre of oven for 50 to 65 minutes. Test by pressing with the fingers. If cooked, cakes should spring back and have begun to shrink from sides of basins. Leave cakes to cool in basins for 5 to 10 minutes, turn out, remove paper and leave the cakes to cool completely on a wire rack.

5. Place coconut in a small basin, add a few drops of green food colouring and mix together until evenly coloured. Spread warmed golden syrup over cake board; sprinkle with green coconut, to represent grass.

6. To make chocolate butter icing: blend cocoa and boiling water together in a basin; reserve 1 × 15ml spoon (1 tablespoon) for the satin icing. Sieve 200g (8oz) icing sugar into a bowl; add 100g (4oz) butter and cocoa mixture. Beat until fluffy. Reserve 1 × 15ml spoon (1 tablespoon).

7. Cut each cake in half horizontally: sandwich halves together with half the remaining chocolate icing. Trim tops of each cake level, if necessary. Spread flat side of one cake with icing; sandwich cakes together. Place on board; spread remaining icing over cake to form a ball.

8. To make satin icing: heat margarine, lemon juice and 2 × 10ml spoons (1½ tablespoons) water in a medium saucepan until margarine has melted. Sift icing sugar. Add 150g (6oz) icing sugar and stir over a low heat until sugar has dissolved; heat for 2 minutes, when mixture should begin to boil gently. (Do not boil syrup quickly, or icing will be too hard to work.) Remove from heat and add 150g (6oz) icing sugar. Beat with a wooden spoon, then pour into a bowl and beat well, scraping down mixture from side of bowl. Gradually add sufficient icing sugar to make the consistency of soft dough. Turn out on to a board dusted with icing sugar. Knead well until icing becomes smooth and white. Divide the icing into 2; place one piece in a well sealed polythene bag. Knead the blended, reserved cocoa into remaining piece, until evenly coloured.

9. Sprinkle a board with cornflour. Roll out brown satin icing thinly. Using a sharp knife, cut into 1.3cm (½in) squares; reserve trimmings, knead together and return to bag. Repeat with the white icing.

10. Carefully lay the squares, alternately, on to butter-iced cake, covering completely, and trimming to fit, where necessary, so that it resembles the patchwork leather (see picture on page 16). With a skewer, mark 2 lines of 3 holes at top of cake for lace holes. Roll a little of remaining white satin icing into a 10cm (4in) lace. Cut into 4 and press the laces into holes. Brush any cornflour from the icing with a pastry brush.

11. Knead white and brown reserved icings separately; form into 6 small footballs. Stick on to board around cake, with golden syrup; press a candle into each ball.

FOOTBALL CAKE *Recipe on page 15*

FIRE ENGINE CAKE *Recipe on page 18*

Fire Engine Cake

(pictured on page 17)

Mrs Jennifer Phillips, from Devizes in Wiltshire, made this cake for her son's second birthday.

METRIC	IMPERIAL
CAKE	**CAKE**
6 × 15ml spoons golden syrup	6 level tablespoons golden syrup
2 × 15ml spoons black treacle	2 level tablespoons black treacle
7 × 15ml spoons oil	7 tablespoons oil
100g soft brown sugar	4oz soft brown sugar
125ml milk	¼ pint milk
175g plain flour	7oz plain flour
25g cocoa	1oz cocoa
1 × 2.5ml spoon bicarbonate of soda	½ level teaspoon bicarbonate of soda
1 × 2.5ml spoon salt	½ level teaspoon salt
1 egg	1 egg
BUTTER ICING	**BUTTER ICING**
200g icing sugar	8oz icing sugar
100g soft margarine	4oz soft margarine
4 drops vanilla essence	4 drops vanilla essence
Red food colouring	Red food colouring
DECORATION	**DECORATION**
50g desiccated coconut	2oz desiccated coconut
Green food colouring	Green food colouring
1 (25cm) square silver cake board	1 (10in) square silver cake board
2 × 15ml spoons golden syrup	1 rounded tablespoon golden syrup
1 (256g) packet liquorice allsorts	1 (9oz) packet liquorice allsorts
6 individual chocolate-coated Swiss rolls	6 individual chocolate-coated Swiss rolls
6 small round biscuits	6 small round biscuits
2 bell-shaped yellow jelly sweets	2 bell-shaped yellow jelly sweets
5 liquorice coils	5 liquorice coils
2 small dairy milk chocolate bars	2 small dairy milk chocolate bars
Red and yellow candles	Red and yellow candles

1. To make cake: prepare a cool oven (150 deg C, 300 deg F, Gas Mark 2). Brush a 1kg (2lb), 1½ litre (3 pint) loaf tin with melted fat. Line base with greaseproof paper; grease paper.

2. Measure golden syrup and treacle carefully, levelling off spoon with a knife and making sure there is none on underside of spoon. Place in a medium-sized saucepan, with oil, brown sugar and milk.

3. Heat gently, stirring until sugar has dissolved; cool.

4. Sift flour, cocoa, bicarbonate of soda and salt into a bowl. Add ingredients from saucepan, and egg. Mix together with a wooden spoon; beat until smooth.

5. Pour mixture into tin; bake in centre of oven for 1

hour to 1 hour 15 minutes. Test by pressing with the fingers. If cooked, the cake should spring back and have begun to shrink from sides of tin. Leave to cool in tin for 15 minutes. Loosen edges with a round-ended knife; turn out, remove paper. Cool on a wire rack.

6. To make butter icing: sift icing sugar into a bowl. Add margarine and vanilla essence; beat together until light and fluffy. Place 2 × 15ml spoons (1 rounded tablespoon) of butter icing in a greaseproof paper piping bag, fitted with a No 1 plain piping tube. Colour remaining butter icing deep red.

7. Toast half the coconut in grill pan until golden brown; cool. Colour remaining coconut green.

8. Brush cake board with warmed golden syrup. Sprinkle a 13cm (5in) wide strip of toasted coconut diagonally across cake board, to represent road. Fill in corners with green coconut, to represent grass.

9. Cut 4 pink and white and 4 orange and white liquorice sweets in halves through the liquorice band; place along edge of grass, coloured sides uppermost, to form kerb stones. Place 3 chocolate rolls on road as supports for engine. Cut 3 remaining chocolate rolls across in halves. Place 1 half next to each whole chocolate roll, so that supports cover width of road.

10. Place cake, base uppermost, on a board; spread sides and top with red butter icing. Sandwich the 3 remaining halved chocolate rolls together; press on to one end of cake, to form bonnet of engine. Cover with remaining red butter icing; spread evenly with a palette knife. Carefully lift engine body on to supports, making sure that one support is underneath the bonnet.

11. To decorate: pipe doors, windows, handles and radiator grille on to fire engine with plain butter icing. Pipe lines on biscuits, to form wheel spokes and place one at each end of supports. Place 2 bell-shaped yellow jelly sweets on top of cab, to represent bells.

12. Place 2 liquorice coils on each side of fire engine. Cut 4 thin yellow slices from a liquorice sweet and place one at the end of each liquorice coil into strips and place in position on cake for bumpers and hubs.

13. Place 5 yellow, black and white layer sweets on top of fire engine behind the bells, and 4 liquorice roll sweets near back of engine. Pipe lines of plain butter icing on to bases of chocolate bars, to form ladders and place on top of liquorice roll and layer sweets. Cut 1 white and liquorice tube sweet in half; position as headlights.

14. Make a small hole in centre of pink and yellow round sweets with liquorice in centres; insert a candle into each sweet and place on corner of cake board.

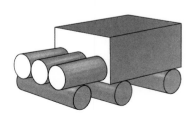

Jason's Dolly

(pictured on page 20)

Mrs A Nicholls, a pharmacist from Worthing, Sussex, sent us the recipe for her son's favourite birthday cake.

METRIC	IMPERIAL
1 × 15ml spoon cocoa	1 level tablespoon cocoa
1 × 15ml spoon boiling water	1 tablespoon boiling water
200g icing sugar	8oz icing sugar
100g butter or margarine	4oz butter or margarine
1 (20cm) round silver cake board	1 (8in) round silver cake board
50g non-pareils	2oz non-pareils
50g chocolate vermicelli	2oz chocolate vermicelli
1 large chocolate-coated Swiss roll	1 large chocolate-coated Swiss roll
3 mini chocolate-coated Swiss rolls	3 mini chocolate-coated Swiss rolls
2 sponge finger biscuits	2 sponge finger biscuits
2 dolly mixture sweets	2 dolly mixture sweets
8 chocolate beans	8 chocolate beans
1 marshmallow	1 marshmallow
Small candles with holders	Small candles with holders

1. Blend cocoa and boiling water together in a basin. Sift icing sugar into a bowl; beat in butter or margarine.
2. Place 1 rounded 5ml spoon (teaspoon) icing in a paper piping bag without a tube. Fold down top. Place two rounded 15ml spoons (tablespoons) of the icing in a paper piping bag fitted with a small star tube. Add cocoa mixture to remaining icing and beat until evenly mixed.
3. Spread a little chocolate icing over cake board. Cut a strip of greaseproof paper 20cm × 5cm (8in × 2in). Draw 2 parallel wavy lines down length of strip; cut along drawn lines. Place strip 2.5cm (1in) in from front edge of board and sprinkle non-pareils over icing. Carefully peel off paper and place approximately 2.5cm (1in) in from first line; sprinkle icing with chocolate vermicelli. Continue with alternate lines of non-pareils and chocolate vermicelli until board is covered.
4. Place remaining chocolate butter icing in a paper piping bag fitted with a small star tube.
5. Cut a 2.5cm (1in) slice from one end of large Swiss roll. Place roll, cut end uppermost, upright on board to form body. Place two mini rolls on board in position for legs. Pipe straight lines of chocolate icing to cover legs, and lower one third of body.
6. Cut a 2.5cm (1in) slice from one end of each sponge finger biscuit; reserve small pieces. Press cut ends of biscuits into each side of body, above legs, to form arms. Pipe chocolate icing in a zig-zag pattern over arms, leaving ends free of icing to represent hands.
7. Place slice of large Swiss roll on top of body, chocolate-coated side to the front, to represent face. Support head with reserved pieces of biscuits. Pipe small whirls of chocolate icing around face and at back of head for hair and for beard. Snip end of piping bag without tube and pipe two circles on face for eyes; press a dolly mixture sweet in centre of each. Pipe a line for mouth, and a dot for dimple on chin.
8. Pipe a zig-zag of white icing up centre of body and a collar below head around top of Swiss roll.
9. Cut each chocolate bean in half and place three pairs on white icing on front of dolly and five halves at end of each leg. Cut marshmallow in half and press one half at end of each leg to represent feet.
10. Press the appropriate number of candles into a slice of remaining mini roll and place on board.

Saffron Cake

(pictured on page 21)

Mrs Jean Toms, a reader from Polruan in Cornwall, finds this traditional Cornish cake very popular with her sons.

METRIC	IMPERIAL
1 × 5ml spoon sugar	1 level teaspoon sugar
125ml hand-hot water (55 deg C)	¼ pint hand-hot water (110 deg F)
1 × 10ml spoon dried yeast	2 level teaspoons dried yeast
5 grains saffron strands	5 grains saffron strands
450g plain flour	1lb plain flour
1 × 2.5ml spoon salt	½ level teaspoon salt
75g lard	3oz lard
75g butter	3oz butter
100g castor sugar	4oz castor sugar
150g currants and sultanas, mixed	6oz currants and sultanas, mixed
25g mixed cut peel	1oz mixed cut peel
Milk	Milk

1. Dissolve 1 × 5ml spoon (1 level teaspoon) sugar in 125ml (¼ pint) hand-hot water and sprinkle yeast on top; leave until frothy, about 10 minutes.
2. Dry saffron in a cool oven; crush with the back of a teaspoon. Place in a measuring jug and pour on 125ml (¼ pint) boiling water; leave to cool.
3. Place flour and salt in a bowl. Add fats, cut into small pieces and rub in with the fingertips, until mixture resembles fine breadcrumbs. Stir in sugar, fruit and mixed peel. Make a well in centre; add saffron water and yeast. Mix with a wooden spoon; beat well until dough leaves side of bowl clean. Cover with greased foil or polythene and leave in a warm place to rise, about 2 hours.
4. Mix dough with a wooden spoon. Turn into a greased, deep round 20cm (8in) cake tin. Cover with greased foil or polythene; leave until risen to top of tin.
5. Prepare a moderate oven (190 deg C, 375 deg F, Gas Mark 5). Brush cake with milk and bake just below centre of oven for 1¼ to 1¾ hours, until cake has shrunk slightly from side of tin and crust is deep golden brown. Leave to cool in tin for 5 minutes, then turn out and leave to cool completely on a wire rack.

Note: alternatively use fresh yeast. Blend 25g (½ oz) fresh yeast with 125ml (¼ pint) warm water. Omit 1 × 5ml spoon (1 teaspoon) sugar and use at once.

20

SAFFRON CAKE *Recipe on page 19*

Elsmore Fudge Flan

(pictured on page 20)

Mrs Janet Elsmore, of Farnham, Surrey, shares with us a secret recipe that has been a favourite with her since she was a child.

For 6 portions

METRIC	IMPERIAL
100g plain flour	4oz plain flour
½ × 2.5ml spoon salt	¼ level teaspoon salt
25g lard	1oz lard
25g margarine	1oz margarine
Cold water to mix	Cold water to mix

FILLING	FILLING
100g soft margarine	4oz soft margarine
100g castor sugar	4oz castor sugar
150g dried skimmed milk	6oz dried skimmed milk
25g drinking chocolate	1oz drinking chocolate
100g sultanas	4oz sultanas

ICING	ICING
25g flaked almonds	1oz flaked almonds
25g glacé cherries	1oz glacé cherries
50g icing sugar	2oz icing sugar
Hot water	Hot water

1. Prepare a moderately hot oven (200 deg C, 400 deg F, Gas Mark 6).
2. Place flour and salt in a bowl. Add fats, cut into small pieces, and rub in with the fingertips until mixture resembles fine breadcrumbs.
3. Add about 1 × 15ml spoon (1 tablespoon) water and mix with a fork to form a firm dough. Turn out on to a floured board and knead lightly.
4. Place an 18cm (7in) fluted flan ring on a baking sheet. Roll out pastry to a circle, 4cm (1½in) larger all round than flan ring. Gently ease pastry into flan ring and press into base and flutes with the fingers. Roll off surplus pastry with rolling pin; press pastry into flutes again. Prick base with a fork.
5. Line flan case with a large circle of greaseproof paper. Half fill with baking beans or rice. Bake just above centre of oven for 15 minutes, to set pastry. Remove paper and beans or rice; cook flan for a further 5 to 10 minutes, until golden brown. Remove flan ring; leave to cool on a wire rack.
6. Cream margarine and sugar together until light and fluffy. Add milk and drinking chocolate, and mix together.
7. Add sultanas and 3 to 4 × 15ml spoons (3 to 4 tablespoons) warm water; mix together. Spread mixture evenly into flan case.
8. Brown almonds under a medium grill. Roughly chop cherries. Sift icing sugar into a basin and stir in sufficient hot water until icing just coats back of spoon. Using a 5ml spoon (1 teaspoon), drizzle icing in a zig-zag pattern over top of flan. Sprinkle with almonds and cherries.

Brentwood Coconut Squares

(pictured on page 20)

Mrs Peterson, from Brentwood, Essex, sent us this recipe which is a hit with everyone at her bridge club.

Makes 30

METRIC	IMPERIAL
150g plain chocolate	6oz plain chocolate
100g glacé cherries	4oz glacé cherries
100g sultanas	4oz sultanas
100g soft margarine	4oz soft margarine
150g castor sugar	6oz castor sugar
2 eggs	2 eggs
200g desiccated coconut	8oz desiccated coconut

1. Prepare a moderate oven (180 deg C, 350 deg F, Gas Mark 4). Brush a 23cm × 33cm (9in × 13in) Swiss roll tin with melted fat or oil. Line base with greaseproof paper; grease paper.
2. Break up chocolate; place in a small dry basin over a saucepan of hot, but not boiling, water. Stir occasionally until chocolate has melted. Remove basin from heat. Spread chocolate evenly over paper on base of tin. Leave in refrigerator until chocolate has hardened.
3. Wash cherries; chop. Chop sultanas. Cream the margarine and sugar together until light and fluffy. Beat eggs and add gradually, beating well after each addition. Add cherries, sultanas and coconut; mix well. Spread mixture evenly over chocolate in tin.
4. Bake in centre of oven for 25 to 35 minutes, until golden brown. Remove from oven and leave until completely cold, to allow chocolate to harden. Cut into five lengthwise, then into six across lengths.

Bess's Gingerbread Snaps

(pictured on page 20)

Miss Bess Torry, from Guernsey, Channel Islands, remembers her mother making these biscuits.

Makes 24 biscuits

METRIC	IMPERIAL
6 × 15ml level spoons black treacle	6 level tablespoons black treacle
75 butter	3oz butter
50g soft brown sugar (light)	2oz soft brown sugar (light)
200g plain flour	8oz plain flour
1 × 2.5ml spoon ground ginger	½ level teaspoon ground ginger
1 × 2.5ml spoon ground	½ level teaspoon ground

coriander	coriander
½ × 2.5ml spoon bicarbonate of soda	¼ level teaspoon bicarbonate of soda
Desiccated coconut	Desiccated coconut
Demerara sugar	Demerara sugar
Castor sugar	Castor sugar
Rolled oats	Rolled oats
Glacé cherries	Glacé cherries
Flaked almonds	Flaked almonds

1. Measure treacle carefully, levelling off spoon with a knife and making sure there is none on underside of spoon; place in a small saucepan. Add butter and sugar and stir over a low heat until butter has melted. Remove pan from the heat. Prepare a moderate oven (180 deg C, 350 deg F, Gas Mark 4).

2. Sift flour, ginger, coriander and bicarbonate of soda into a bowl. Add melted mixture and mix. Leave to cool slightly. Brush two baking sheets with melted fat.

3. Turn out mixture on to a board. Cut mixture in two. Roll each half into a roll, 30cm (12in) long. Cut each roll into 12. Roll each piece into a ball.

4. Place some coconut, demerara sugar and castor sugar, or rolled oats on to separate plates. Roll some biscuits in each, to coat, then place on baking sheets a little apart to allow for spreading. Flatten slightly. Leave other biscuits plain and press halved glacé cherries or flaked almonds on to flattened biscuits.

5. Bake in centre and just above centre of oven for 8 to 10 minutes. Leave to cool on baking sheets for 2 minutes; remove and leave to cool on a wire rack.

Bonfire Cake

Mrs G Sharp, from Sandwich in Kent, made this cake for a bonfire birthday party.

METRIC	IMPERIAL
CAKE	CAKE
150g soft margarine	6oz soft margarine
150g castor sugar	6oz castor sugar
3 eggs	3 eggs
150g self-raising flour	6oz self-raising flour
50g cornflour	1½oz cornflour
3 × 2.5ml spoons baking powder	1½ level teaspoons baking powder
Strawberry essence	Strawberry essence
Red food colouring	Red food colouring
ICING	ICING
200g icing sugar	8oz icing sugar
100g butter	4oz butter
1 × 15ml spoon milk	1 tablespoon milk
Red food colouring	Red food colouring
DECORATION	DECORATION
1 (20cm) round silver cake board	1 (8in) round silver cake board
6 chocolate flake bars	6 chocolate flake bars
75g marzipan	3oz marzipan
Green and red food colouring	Green and red food colouring
Candles	Candles

1. To make cake: prepare a moderate oven (170 deg C, 325 deg F, Gas Mark 3). Brush a ¾ litre (1½ pint) ovenglass pudding basin with melted fat or oil. Line base with greaseproof paper; grease paper.

2. Place margarine, castor sugar, eggs, flour, cornflour and baking powder in a bowl. Mix with wooden spoon; beat for 1 to 2 minutes, until mixture is smooth.

3. Place half the mixture in a basin; add 1 × 5ml spoon (1 teaspoon) strawberry essence. Stir in a few drops of red food colouring; mix until evenly coloured.

4. Place alternate 15ml spoonsful (tablespoonsful) of plain and coloured mixture in prepared basin; level top.

5. Bake on shelf in centre of oven for 55 to 65 minutes. Test by pressing with the fingers. If cooked, cake should spring back and have begun to shrink from side of basin.

6. Leave to cool in basin for 5 to 10 minutes. Loosen edges with a round-ended knife, turn out, remove paper and leave to cool completely on a wire rack.

7. To make icing: sift icing sugar into a bowl. Add butter and milk; beat together until light and fluffy. Add few drops red colouring; mix until evenly coloured.

8. Cut cake into 3 layers; sandwich together with a little butter icing. Cover cake completely with remaining icing. Form a peak on top. Place cake on board.

9. Cut each chocolate flake bar into 4 lengthwise; stick pieces on cake, to represent firewood.

10. To make guy doll: divide marzipan into 3. Knead a drop of green colouring into 1 piece and a drop of red colouring into another. Cut green marzipan into 3. Roll 1 piece into a ball for crown of hat and press out another piece to a 3cm (1¼in) circle for brim.

11. Cut red marzipan into 3. Roll 1 piece into a ball for guy's face and gently press under brim of hat. Roll another red piece into oblong body; press under head.

12. Divide plain marzipan into 4. Roll 1 piece into an oblong; snip at each side, to make a feather. Place around brim of hat. Divide another piece into small balls for features on guy's face. Roll another piece and press out to form a collar. Place guy on top of cake.

13. Form fireworks with remaining marzipan; place on board around cake. Stick candles into fireworks.

Left: sandwich layers and form a peak. Right: chocolate flake represents wood.

23

Ground Rice Cake

Mrs Betty Kerr, one of our readers from Brockweir in Gloucestershire, had this recipe handed down to her from her great grandmother.

METRIC	IMPERIAL
100g butter or margarine	4oz butter or margarine
100g castor sugar	4oz castor sugar
2 eggs	2 eggs
1 × 2.5ml spoon vanilla essence	½ teaspoon vanilla essence
75g ground rice	3oz ground rice
25g self-raising flour	1oz self-raising flour
½ × 2.5ml spoon salt	¼ level teaspoon salt

1. Prepare a moderate oven (190 deg C, 375 deg F, Gas Mark 5). Brush an 18cm (7in) sandwich tin with melted fat or oil. Line base and side with greaseproof paper; grease paper.
2. Cream butter or margarine and sugar together in a bowl, until light and fluffy. Beat eggs, 1 × 15ml spoon (1 tablespoon) water and vanilla essence together and then add gradually, beating after each addition. Fold in ground rice, flour and salt with a metal spoon.
3. Spread mixture evenly in tin and smooth top with back of metal spoon. Bake in centre of oven for 20 to 30 minutes.
4. Test by pressing with the fingers. If cooked, cake should spring back and have begun to shrink from side of tin. Leave in tin until cold, then loosen edges with a knife, turn out and remove paper; store in a tin.
Note: this ground rice cake will actually improve in flavour if you store it for up to 4 weeks in a closed tin.

Melting Moments

(pictured below)

Mrs Eileen Marsh, from Ashby-de-la-Zouch, won a prize with this recipe in a Reader Club competition.

Makes about 20

METRIC	IMPERIAL
75g lard	2½oz lard
25g margarine	1½oz margarine
75g castor sugar	3oz castor sugar
Half an egg	Half an egg
1 × 5ml spoon vanilla essence	1 teaspoon vanilla essence
125g self-raising flour	5oz self-raising flour
25g rolled (porridge) oats	1oz rolled (porridge) oats
10 glacé cherries	10 glacé cherries

1. Prepare a moderate oven (180 deg C, 350 deg F, Gas Mark 4). Grease 2 baking sheets.
2. Place fats and sugar in a bowl; beat together with a wooden spoon until light and fluffy. Beat egg with vanilla essence; add to creamed mixture, a little at a time, beating well after each addition. Fold in flour, to form a soft dough.
3. Roll into walnut-sized balls with wet hands, then dip in rolled oats, to coat.
4. Place on baking sheets, a little apart to allow for spreading; press out slightly. Top each melting moment with half a glacé cherry.
5. Bake just above and below centre of oven for 15 to 20 minutes, until pale golden brown. Leave to cool on baking sheets for 5 minutes, then remove and leave to cool completely on a wire rack. Store in a closed tin.

MELTING MOMENTS

Orange Biscuits

Mrs Ann Sandford, from Exeter in Devon, sent us her favourite recipe.

Makes about 40

METRIC	IMPERIAL
200g self-raising flour	8oz self-raising flour
125g margarine	5oz margarine
Castor sugar	Castor sugar
Grated rind of 2 medium-sized oranges	Grated rind of 2 medium-sized oranges
1 egg	1 egg
1 × 15ml spoon milk	1 tablespoon milk

1. Prepare a moderate oven (190 deg C, 375 deg F, Gas Mark 5). Grease 2 baking sheets.
2. Place flour in a bowl. Add margarine, cut into small pieces and rub in with the fingertips until mixture resembles fine breadcrumbs. Mix in 125g (5oz) castor sugar and orange rind.
3. Separate egg; place white in a small basin and beat lightly with a fork. Beat egg yolk and milk together; add to dry ingredients in bowl. Mix to form a firm dough.
4. Turn out on to a floured board and knead until smooth. Roll out thinly, brush dough with egg white and sprinkle lightly with castor sugar.
5. Cut into rounds with a 5cm (2in) fluted cutter. Knead together trimmings and roll out, to make more rounds. Repeat brushing with egg white and sprinkling with sugar. Place biscuits on baking sheets, a little apart, to allow for spreading.
6. Bake just above and below centre of oven for 12 to 15 minutes, until biscuits are pale golden brown. Remove from baking sheets and leave to cool on a wire rack. Store in an airtight container.

Fruit and Honey Cookies

These nut-topped cookies are firm favourites with reader Mrs Susan Gater, and her family, who come from Bristol.

Makes about 40

METRIC	IMPERIAL
100g margarine	4oz margarine
100g soft brown sugar (light)	4oz soft brown sugar (light)
2 × 15ml spoons clear honey	2 level tablespoons clear honey
1 egg	1 egg
50g mixed dried fruit (raisins, currants, sultanas)	2oz mixed dried fruit (raisins, currants, sultanas)
200g self-raising flour	8oz self-raising flour
1 × 2.5ml spoon salt	½ level teaspoon salt
50g shelled walnuts	2oz shelled walnuts

1. Prepare a moderate oven (180 deg C, 350 deg F, Gas Mark 4). Grease 2 baking sheets.
2. Cream margarine and sugar together until light and fluffy. Measure honey carefully, levelling off spoon with a knife and making sure there is none on underside of spoon. Add to bowl; mix well. Beat egg and add gradually, beating well after each addition. Add dried fruit and mix well. Stir in flour and salt, until a stiff dough is formed.
3. Form mixture into balls, each the size of a walnut. Roughly chop nuts; place on a saucer. Dip one side of each cookie in nuts; press lightly. Place cookies with their nut-covered sides uppermost, on to the prepared baking sheets.
4. Bake just above and below centre of oven for 12 to 15 minutes, until golden brown. Leave to cool on baking sheets for 1 minute, then remove and leave to cool completely on a wire rack. Store cookies in an airtight container to keep them fresh.

Date Shorties

This recipe was given to us by Mrs Susan Burnell, from Yeovil in Somerset.

Makes 16

METRIC	IMPERIAL
FILLING	FILLING
200g dates	½lb dates
1 lemon	1 lemon
CRUMBLE MIXTURE	CRUMBLE MIXTURE
100g plain flour	4oz plain flour
100g semolina	4oz semolina
75g butter or margarine	3oz butter or margarine
75g castor sugar	3oz castor sugar
Granulated sugar	Granulated sugar

1. Prepare a moderate oven (190 deg C, 375 deg F, Gas Mark 5). Grease a 28cm by 18cm by 4cm deep (11in by 7in by 1½in deep) tin.
2. Chop dates; place in a saucepan. Scrub lemon; grate rind and squeeze juice into a measuring jug. Make up to 250ml (½ pint) with cold water; add liquid to dates in saucepan. Cook until the dates are soft and pulpy; leave to cool.
3. Place flour and semolina in a bowl. Add butter or margarine, cut into small pieces and rub in with the fingertips until mixture resembles fine breadcrumbs; stir in castor sugar.
4. Press half the crumble mixture evenly over base of tin; spread with date mixture. Cover with remaining crumble mixture; press down lightly.
5. Bake in centre of oven for 20 to 30 minutes, until pale golden brown. Sprinkle with a little granulated sugar. Leave in tin until cold. Cut along length into 2, then across into 8 to make 16 bars; remove shorties from the tin and store in an airtight container to keep them fresh.

Chocolate Fingers

Mrs Angela West, from Maidstone in Kent, sent us the idea for this recipe.

Makes 7 biscuits

METRIC	IMPERIAL
50g plain chocolate	2oz plain chocolate
1 × 15ml spoon milk	1 tablespoon milk
1 packet (14) sponge finger biscuits	1 packet (14) sponge finger biscuits
50g icing sugar	2oz icing sugar
25g butter	1oz butter

1. Grate a 5ml spoonful (teaspoonful) of chocolate; reserve for decoration.
2. Break up remaining chocolate; place, with milk, in a small, dry basin over a small saucepan of hot, but not boiling, water. Stir occasionally until chocolate has melted. Remove basin from saucepan.
3. Dip one end of each finger biscuit in the chocolate; drain for a moment, then leave on a wire rack to harden.
4. Sift icing sugar into a bowl. Add butter and beat together until light and fluffy. Beat in any remaining melted chocolate.
5. Sandwich biscuits together with chocolate butter icing, using a small star icing tube, if desired. Sprinkle with the grated chocolate.

Strawberry Meringue Gâteau

(pictured on cover)

This recipe, for the strawberry season, comes from Mrs Joy Howard, of Bridport in Dorset.

For 6 to 8 portions

METRIC	IMPERIAL
Castor sugar	Castor sugar
100g margarine	4oz margarine
3 eggs	3 eggs
Milk	Milk
100g self-raising flour	4oz self-raising flour
¼kg strawberries	½lb strawberries
200ml double cream	7 fluid oz double cream

1. Prepare a moderate oven (180 deg C, 350 deg F, Gas Mark 4). Brush 2, 20cm (8in) sandwich tins with melted fat. Line bases and sides of tins with greaseproof paper; grease paper.
2. Place 100g (4oz) castor sugar and margarine in a bowl; beat together until light and fluffy.
3. Separate 2 eggs; place whites in clean, grease-free basin and beat yolks with remaining whole egg and 1 × 15ml spoon (1 tablespoon) milk into creamed mixture.
4. Fold flour into creamed mixture with a metal spoon. Divide mixture between tins and level tops with back of spoon.
5. Whisk the egg whites until stiff, but not dry. Whisk in 50g (2oz) castor sugar and then carefully fold

in another 50g (2oz) castor sugar with a metal spoon.
6. Place one third of meringue in a nylon piping bag fitted with a medium-sized star tube. Spread remaining meringue over mixture in each tin. Pipe a row of stars around edge of one of the cakes.
7. Place cakes in centre of oven and cook for 40 to 45 minutes, until meringue is well risen and golden brown. Leave to cool in tins for 15 minutes, then carefully remove cakes from tins and leave to cool completely on a wire rack; remove paper.
8. Wash strawberries; reserve 8 whole strawberries for decoration. Hull and slice remainder.
9. Whisk cream and 2 × 15ml spoons (2 tablespoons) milk until just thick; spread about two thirds over unpiped base, and top with the sliced strawberries. Place piped layer on top. Pile remaining cream in centre and decorate with reserved strawberries.

Australian Sponge Cake

See if you're as impressed as we were with this recipe from Mrs Lorna Hodge, of Moreton-on-Lugg, Hertfordshire.

METRIC	IMPERIAL
4 eggs	4 eggs
Pinch of salt	Pinch of salt
1 × 2.5ml spoon vanilla essence	½ teaspoon vanilla essence
150g castor sugar	6oz castor sugar
75g cornflour	3oz cornflour
1 × 10ml spoon plain flour	1 rounded teaspoon plain flour
3 × 10ml spoons self-raising flour	3 rounded teaspoons self-raising flour
1 × 2.5ml spoon bicarbonate of soda	½ level teaspoon bicarbonate of soda
1 × 5ml spoon cream of tartar	1 level teaspoon cream of tartar
150ml double cream	¼ pint double cream
Raspberry jam	Raspberry jam
Icing sugar	Icing sugar

1. Prepare a moderate oven (190 deg C, 375 deg F, Gas Mark 5). Brush 2, 20cm (8in) sandwich tins with melted fat. Line bases with greaseproof paper; grease paper.
2. Place eggs, salt, vanilla essence and castor sugar in a bowl. Whisk together until mixture leaves a trail.
3. Sift cornflour, plain flour, self-raising flour, bicarbonate of soda and cream of tartar together, then carefully fold into egg mixture with a metal spoon, cutting through the mixture until all has been incorporated.
4. Pour into prepared tins and cook in centre of oven for 25 to 35 minutes. Test by pressing with the fingers. If cooked, cake should spring back, and have begun to shrink from sides of tins.
5. Turn out on a wire rack, remove paper; leave to cool.
6. Place cream in a basin and whisk until just thick. Sandwich cakes together with a little raspberry jam and cream. Dredge top of sponge with some icing sugar.

26

Cornflake Macaroons

Mrs Susan Jones, from Cardiff, finds Cornflake Macaroons are top favourites with her children.

Makes about 30

METRIC	IMPERIAL
50g cornflakes	2oz cornflakes
50g blanched almonds	2oz blanched almonds
2 egg whites	2 egg whites
175g castor sugar	7oz castor sugar
1 × 15ml spoon clear honey	1 level tablespoon clear honey
75g desiccated coconut	3oz desiccated coconut
1 × 2.5ml spoon almond essence	½ teaspoon almond essence

1. Prepare a cool oven (150 deg C, 300 deg F, Gas Mark 2). Grease 2 baking sheets.
2. Place cornflakes in a paper bag; crush with the hands. chop almonds. Place egg whites in a clean, grease-free bowl and whisk until stiff, but not dry.
3. Fold in sugar with a metal spoon. Measure honey carefully, levelling off spoon with a knife and making sure there is none on underside. Fold into mixture with cornflakes, almonds, coconut and almond essence.
4. Pile heaped 5ml spoonsful (teaspoonsful) of mixture on to baking sheets, about 2.5cm (1in) apart.
5. Bake just above and below centre of oven for 15 to 25 minutes, until pale golden brown. Leave to cool on baking sheets for 1 to 2 minutes. Remove with a palette knife and leave to cool completely on a wire rack.

Chocolate Coconut Delight

Stephen Mardon, from The Vicarage, Cullompton, Devon, sent us this, his favourite, recipe.

Makes 16

METRIC	IMPERIAL
75g chocolate-flavour cake covering	3oz chocolate-flavour cake covering
50g unsalted peanuts	2oz unsalted peanuts
50g currants	2oz currants
50g sultanas	2oz sultanas
75g desiccated coconut	3oz desiccated coconut
4 × 15ml spoons sweetened condensed milk	2 rounded tablespoons sweetened condensed milk
150g granulated sugar	6oz granulated sugar

1. Brush a shallow, 18cm (7in) square tin with melted fat or oil. Line base with greaseproof paper.
2. Place chocolate covering in a small, dry basin over a saucepan of hot, but not boiling, water. Stir occasionally until chocolate is melted; remove basin from saucepan.
3. Pour the chocolate cake covering into tin; spread evenly over the base.
4. Place peanuts in a bowl; cover with boiling water. Leave for 1 minute; drain, remove skins and split peanuts in halves.
5. Place peanuts in a bowl; add currants, sultanas, coconut and condensed milk. Mix with a wooden spoon.
6. Spread mixture over chocolate in tin; level top.
7. Place sugar in a small saucepan; place over a moderate heat, until sugar melts and turns a rich golden brown. Remove saucepan from heat; quickly pour sugar over coconut mixture, tilting tin to cover top evenly.
8. Quickly mark into 16 squares with an oiled knife, before caramel sets.
9. Loosen edge of mixture with a palette knife; turn mixture out of tin and remove paper. Cut along marked lines into 16 squares and arrange on a serving plate. Serve them on the same day they are made.

Banana Cake

Mrs Gaye Faber, from Chester, provided us with this tempting recipe.

METRIC	IMPERIAL
CAKE	CAKE
1 egg	1 egg
50g soft margarine	2oz soft margarine
50g castor sugar	2oz castor sugar
1 medium-sized banana	1 medium-sized banana
1 × 2.5ml spoon vanilla essence	½ teaspoon vanilla essence
125g self-raising flour	5oz self-raising flour
½ × 2.5ml spoon bicarbonate of soda	¼ level teaspoon bicarbonate of soda
½ × 2.5ml spoon salt	¼ level teaspoon salt
FILLING	FILLING
2 medium-sized bananas	2 medium-sized bananas
1 × 10ml spoon lemon juice	2 teaspoons lemon juice
Icing sugar	Icing sugar

1. Prepare a moderate oven (190 deg C, 375 deg F, Gas Mark 5). Brush an 18cm (7in) sandwich tin with melted fat. Line base with greaseproof paper; grease paper.
2. Place egg, margarine and castor sugar in a liquidiser goblet. Peel banana, cut into pieces and add to goblet with vanilla essence.
3. Blend until smooth. Pour into a bowl. Sift flour, bicarbonate of soda and salt into bowl; fold into mixture.
4. Place mixture in tin; smooth top with back of a metal spoon. Bake in centre of oven for 25 to 35 minutes. Test by pressing with the fingers. If cooked, cake should spring back and have begun to shrink from side of tin. Leave to cool in tin for 5 minutes. Turn out, remove paper and leave to cool. To make filling: peel 2 bananas, cut into thin slices. Toss in lemon juice, to coat.
5. Cut cake into 2 layers; arrange a small circle of overlapping banana slices in centre of top layer of cake.
6. Mash remaining slices; spread evenly over base of cake. Replace top layer and dredge with icing sugar.

What shall we eat tonight? is a midweek headache for so many women. In the following pages you answer the question for one another with meat puddings, stews, pies and quickie dishes, plus tantalising desserts

Chicken Campala

Mrs Mary Morrison, from Paisley, Scotland, was a finalist in one of the Cook of the Year competitions.

For 4 portions

METRIC	IMPERIAL
1 roasting chicken (1½kg drawn weight)	1 roasting chicken (3lb drawn weight)
Salt	Salt
Pepper	Pepper
1 × 5ml spoon dry mustard	1 level teaspoon dry mustard
1 × 2.5ml spoon mixed dried herbs	½ level teaspoon mixed dried herbs
125ml oil	¼ pint oil
100g button mushrooms	4oz button mushrooms
2 medium-sized onions	2 medium-sized onions
100g green grapes	4oz green grapes
4 medium-sized tomatoes	4 medium-sized tomatoes
2 chicken cubes	2 chicken cubes
200g long-grain rice	8oz long-grain rice
2 × 15ml spoons plain flour	2 level tablespoons plain flour
1 small can evaporated milk	1 small can evaporated milk
1 to 2 × 15ml spoons sherry	1 to 2 tablespoons sherry

1. Remove giblets and rinse inside of chicken with cold water; dry thoroughly with kitchen paper. Place chicken on a board. Using a large, sharp knife, cut through backbone of chicken, turn over and cut through breastbone, to cut chicken in half.
2. Lay each chicken half flat; cut off end of each leg to first joint and discard. Cut each chicken half between wing and leg. Cut off wing tips.
3. Place 1 × 5ml spoon (1 level teaspoon) salt, a shake of pepper, mustard and mixed dried herbs in a basin; mix well. Rub chicken joints with mixture.
4. Heat oil in a frying pan. Fry chicken joints for 20 to 25 minutes, turning chicken occasionally, to cook evenly. Remove and place on a plate; cover and leave to cool. When cool, remove skin and bone from chicken; chop meat.
5. Wash and slice mushrooms. Peel and chop onions. Peel and halve the grapes and remove pips. Place the tomatoes in a basin and cover them with boiling water. Leave for 1 minute; drain, then peel off skins and slice.

6. Heat 2 litres (4 pints) water in a large saucepan; crumble and stir in stock cubes. Pour 250ml (½ pint) stock into a jug and reserve for sauce. Add 1 × 10ml spoon (2 level teaspoons) salt to stock in pan; bring to boil and add rice. Boil rice for about 12 minutes, until tender. Test by pressing a grain between thumb and finger. Drain in a sieve and rinse with boiling water. Arrange rice around edge of a large, warmed, shallow serving dish; keep warm.
7. Drain off all, except 1 × 15ml spoon (1 tablespoon), of oil from pan. Add onion; fry until soft, about 5 minutes. Stir in flour and half of evaporated milk. Add reserved stock and bring to boil, stirring. Stir in mushrooms and chicken pieces; cook gently for 10 minutes. Add sliced tomatoes and grapes; taste and add more salt and pepper, if necessary. Pour in centre of rice in dish.
8. Whisk remaining evaporated milk until thick. Whisk in 1 to 2 × 15ml spoons (1 to 2 tablespoons) sherry, to taste. Pour into a sauce boat and serve with chicken.

Sausage and Egg Pie

(pictured opposite)
Mrs Maureen Briggs makes this delicious dish for summer lunches.

For 4 portions

METRIC	IMPERIAL
1 large (368g) packet frozen puff pastry, just thawed	1 large (13oz) packet of frozen puff pastry, just thawed
¼kg (8) pork chipolata sausages	½lb (8) pork chipolata sausages
4 eggs	4 eggs
4 rashers streaky bacon	4 rashers streaky bacon
1 tomato	1 tomato
Salt and pepper	Salt and pepper
Beaten egg or milk to glaze	Beaten egg or milk, to glaze

1. Prepare a moderately hot oven (200 deg C, 400 deg F, Gas Mark 6).
2. Roll out two thirds of the pastry to a 25cm (10in) circle. Lift pastry over rolling pin and press into a 20cm (8in) sandwich tin, taking care not to stretch pastry; trim edge with a knife.
3. Place 4 sausages around edge of pastry and 4 from

SAUSAGE AND EGG PIE

29

edge to centre, to form a cross, leaving 4 hollows. Crack an egg into each hollow.

4. Remove rind and bone from bacon; cut bacon into strips and place over eggs. Slice tomato into 4; place a slice on each egg yolk. Sprinkle with salt and pepper.

5. Roll out remaining pastry to cover pie. Brush rim of pastry with water. Support pastry on rolling pin and place over filling. Press edges together firmly; trim with a knife. Using the back of knife, cut edge of pastry, to form flakes; flute edge with the fingers.

6. Make a small hole in centre of pie. Brush pie with beaten egg or milk. Roll out pastry trimmings; cut out leaves. Arrange around hole; brush with egg or milk.

7. Cook pie in centre of oven for 15 minutes; reduce heat to cool (170 deg C, 325 deg F, Gas Mark 3) and cook for a further 30 minutes, until pastry is golden brown. Serve hot or cold with salad.

Note: alternatively, use shortcrust pastry, made from 200g (8oz) plain flour.

Cold Weather Stew

Mrs Jean Toms, one of our readers from Polruan in Cornwall, sent us this recipe.

For 4 portions

METRIC	IMPERIAL
½kg stewing steak	1¼lb stewing steak
2 medium-sized onions	2 medium-sized onions
3 large carrots	3 large carrots
1 large turnip	1 large turnip
2 large parsnips	2 large parsnips
25g plain flour	1oz plain flour
1 × 10ml spoon salt	1 rounded teaspoon salt
Pepper	Pepper
25g dripping or lard	1oz dripping or lard
1 beef bone	1 beef bone
Gravy browning (optional)	Gravy browning (optional)

DUMPLINGS	DUMPLINGS
200g self-raising flour	8oz self-raising flour
100g shredded suet	4oz shredded suet
1 × 5ml spoon salt	1 level teaspoon salt
Cold water to mix	Cold water to mix

1. Cut meat into 2cm (1in) cubes, removing excess fat and gristle.

2. Peel and quarter onions. Peel carrots, turnip and parsnips; cut into 2cm (1in) cubes.

3. Mix flour, salt and a shake of pepper together on a plate; coat meat in seasoned flour.

4. Melt dripping or lard in a large saucepan, add meat and fry until browned on all sides. Add any remaining seasoned flour, vegetables, ½ litre (1 pint) water and bone. Bring to boil, stirring; cover and simmer very slowly, stirring occasionally, for 2½ to 3 hours, adding a little more water, if necessary. Colour the stew with a little gravy browning, if desired. Remove the beef bone.

5. To make dumplings; place flour, suet and salt in a bowl. Stir in sufficent water to make a soft, but not sticky, dough. Turn out on to a floured board, then divide into 8 equal pieces; form into balls and place on top of stew. Cover saucepan and cook for a further 15 to 20 minutes, until dumplings are well risen. Serve the stew hot with a green vegetable.

Stuffed Pork Fillet

Mrs Helen Lawrence, one of our readers from Bangor, Northern Ireland, serves this dish when entertaining.

For 4 portions

METRIC	IMPERIAL
¼ to ½kg potatoes	¾lb to 1lb potatoes
50g lard	2oz lard
300g pork fillet	¾lb pork fillet

STUFFING	STUFFING
1 small onion	1 small onion
75g fresh white breadcrumbs	3oz fresh white breadcrumbs
1 × 10ml spoon dried sage	2 level teaspoons dried sage
1 × 5ml spoon salt	1 level teaspoon salt
Pepper	Pepper
1 egg yolk	1 egg yolk
25g plain flour	½oz plain flour
250ml stock or vegetable water	½ pint stock or vegetable water

1. Prepare a moderate oven (190 deg C, 375 deg F, Gas Mark 5).

2. Peel potatoes, cut into medium-sized pieces, place in boiling, salted water and cook for 5 minutes; drain. Melt 25g (1oz) lard in a roasting tin; add potatoes and coat in lard.

3. Split pork fillet lengthwise and flatten out on a board (or ask your butcher to do this for you). Peel and grate onion. Melt remaining 25g (1oz) lard in a saucepan, add onion, breadcrumbs, sage, salt, a shake of pepper and egg yolk; mix well.

4. Spread stuffing on pork fillet and roll up lengthwise. Tie with string at 5cm (2in) intervals along fillet. Place, join side downwards, in roasting tin and baste with lard.

5. Cook in centre of oven for 1 to 1¼ hours until pork is tender. Lift meat and potatoes out on to a warmed serving dish; keep warm. Strain most of the fat from roasting tin. Stir in flour, then add stock or vegetable water. Bring to boil, stirring, and simmer for 3 minutes. Taste and season with salt and pepper, then pour into a warmed gravy boat. Serve with a green vegetable.

Note: if unable to obtain pork fillet, use a 1cm (½in) thick slice of top leg of pork and remove small bone. If a small pork fillet is used, just wrap the pork around the stuffing mixture and cook with stuffing side uppermost.

BACON ROLL

Bacon Roll

(pictured above)

Mrs Brenda Nixon, of Sittingbourne, Kent, and her family enjoy this good, warming British fare.

For 6 portions

METRIC	IMPERIAL
FILLING	FILLING
250g streaky bacon	**½lb streaky bacon**
1 medium-sized onion	**1 medium-sized onion**
Salt and pepper	**Salt and pepper**
SUET PASTRY	SUET PASTRY
350g self-raising flour	**12oz self-raising flour**
175g shredded suet	**6oz shredded suet**
Cold water to mix	**Cold water to mix**

SAUCE	SAUCE
1 (396g) can tomatoes	**1 (14oz) can tomatoes**
1 × 5ml spoon granulated sugar	**1 level teaspoon granulated sugar**
1 × 2.5ml spoon Worcestershire sauce	**½ teaspoon Worcestershire sauce**
Salt and pepper	**Salt and pepper**
Sliced tomato and parsley to garnish	**Sliced tomato and parsley to garnish**

1. Prepare a moderately hot oven (200 deg C, 400 deg F, Gas Mark 6).

2. Remove rind and bone from bacon; chop bacon. Peel and chop onion. Mix bacon, onion and a little salt and pepper together in a basin.

3. Mix together flour and suet in a bowl and add sufficient cold water, about 10 to 12 × 15ml spoons (10 to 12 tablespoons) to make a soft, but not sticky, dough.

4. Turn out on to a floured board and knead lightly. Roll out to a 30cm (12in) square. Place bacon mixture over pastry to within 2cm (1in) of edges. Brush edges with water and roll up; seal ends with the fingers and wrap roll loosely in a piece of foil. Place on a baking sheet and bake in centre of oven for 1¼ to 1½ hours, until pastry is golden brown.

5. Place contents of can of tomatoes, granulated sugar, Worcestershire sauce and a little salt and pepper in a saucepan; bring slowly to boil. Place tomato sauce in a warmed sauce boat.

6. Place bacon roll on a warmed serving dish; place sliced tomato on roll and garnish with sprigs of parsley. Serve with tomato sauce.

Meatballs with Tomato Rice

Mrs Jill Curtis, one of our readers from Bury St Edmunds in Suffolk, finds this recipe a family favourite.

For 4 portions

METRIC	IMPERIAL
100g Cheddar cheese	**4oz Cheddar cheese**
1 small onion	**1 small onion**
1 egg	**1 egg**
½kg minced beef	**1lb minced beef**
2 × 15ml spoons oil	**2 tablespoons oil**
200g long-grain rice	**8oz long-grain rice**
1 (287g) can condensed tomato soup	**1 (10½oz) can condensed tomato soup**
1 × 5ml spoon salt	**1 level teaspoon salt**
Pepper	**Pepper**
½ × 2.5ml spoon dry mustard	**¼ level teaspoon dry mustard**
1 × 2.5ml spoon mixed dried herbs or a shake of garlic salt	**½ level teaspoon mixed dried herbs or a shake of garlic salt**

1. Prepare a moderate oven (180 dec C, 350 deg F, Gas Mark 4).

2. Grate cheese. Peel and chop onion. Beat egg, add cheese and meat and mix well. Turn out on to a floured board and shape into 8 balls.

3. Heat oil in a frying pan and fry meatballs until browned. Lift out and place, with rice, in a 1¾ litre (3½ pint) casserole.

4. Add onion to pan and cook for 2 minutes. Stir in soup, ½ litre (1 pint) water, salt, a shake of pepper, mustard and herbs or garlic salt. Bring to boil, stirring, and pour into casserole. Cover with a lid or foil.

5. Cook in centre of oven for 45 minutes to 1 hour, until the meatballs are tender and the rice has absorbed the liquid. Stir the rice mixture before serving. Serve with sweet corn and sliced green beans.

Braised Steak with Mushrooms

Mrs Rose Hayden, who comes from Brixham in Devon, serves this dish to her guests.

For 4 portions

METRIC	IMPERIAL
½kg braising steak	1¼lb braising steak
100g mushrooms	4oz mushrooms
2 medium-sized onions	2 medium-sized onions
50g lard	1½oz lard
½ × 2.5ml spoon season-all or ½ × 2.5ml spoon salt and a pinch of pepper	¼ level teaspoon season-all or ¼ level teaspoon salt and a pinch of pepper
1 × 5ml spoon paprika	1 level teaspoon paprika
1 × 10ml spoon yeast extract	1 rounded teaspoon yeast extract
250ml boiling water	½ pint boiling water
1 × 10ml spoon cornflour	2 level teaspoons cornflour
1 bay leaf	1 bay leaf

1. Prepare a cool oven (150 deg C, 300 deg F, Gas Mark 2).

2. Trim any excess fat and gristle from steak; cut steak into 4 portions.

3. Wash and slice mushrooms. Peel and slice onions.

4. Melt lard in a large frying pan; fry mushrooms lightly and place in a large, shallow casserole. Add steak to frying pan and fry quickly on each side to seal. Place on mushrooms in casserole. Add onions to frying pan; fry for about 3 minutes, then arrange over steak.

5. Sprinkle meat with season-all (or salt and pepper) and paprika.

6. Dissolve yeast extract in boiling water. Mix cornflour and 1 × 15ml spoon (1 tablespoon) cold water together and stir into yeast extract; pour over meat. Add bay leaf.

7. Cover and cook in centre of oven for 2½ to 3 hours or until meat is tender. Remove bay leaf and serve braised steak with creamed potatoes and a green vegetable.

Cheese and Fish Pie

Try your hand at making this dish, the recipe for which comes from reader, Mrs Mona Hutton, who lives in Inverness, in Scotland.

For 4 portions

METRIC	IMPERIAL
POTATO CASE	POTATO CASE
1kg potatoes	2lb potatoes
Salt and pepper	Salt and pepper
75g butter	2½oz butter
Milk	Milk
FILLING	FILLING
½kg smoked haddock fillet	1lb smoked haddock fillet
Milk	Milk
50g margarine	1½oz margarine
50g plain flour	1½oz plain flour
150g Orkney or red Leicester cheese	6oz Orkney or red Leicester cheese
Parsley to garnish	Parsley to garnish

1. Wash and peel potatoes. Cut into even-sized pieces and place in a saucepan of cold, salted water. Bring to boil, cover and simmer until tender, about 20 minutes.

2. Drain potatoes and toss over a low heat to dry. Sieve potatoes, add some salt and pepper; beat in butter and 4 × 15ml spoons (4 tablespoons) milk.

3. Remove rack from grill pan and prepare a moderate grill. Place potato in a large nylon piping bag, fitted with a large star tube. Pipe potato on base and side of a round, shallow 20cm (8in) ovenproof dish, forming a case. Grill until just golden, then remove from heat.

4. Wash and trim haddock; cut into even-sized pieces. Place fish, with 275ml (½ pint) milk, in a saucepan. Bring to boil; cover and simmer for about 7 minutes, until fish is tender. Remove fish from saucepan, reserving liquid in a measuring jug. Make up to 275ml (½ pint) with milk, if necessary. Remove bones and flake the fish.

5. Melt margarine in a saucepan, stir in flour and cook gently for 2 minutes, without browning. Add fish liquid and bring to boil, stirring continuously. Cook for 2 minutes.

6. Grate cheese; add 100g (4oz) cheese and flaked haddock to sauce. Stir gently until cheese has melted. Pile mixture into potato case and sprinkle with remaining cheese.

7. Return the dish to the grill and cook until cheese is golden brown and bubbling. Garnish with sprigs of parsley and serve with grilled tomatoes.

STEAK AND KIDNEY PIE *Recipe on page 34*

Steak and Kidney Pie

(pictured on page 33)

Mrs Olive Winzer, from Exmoor, Devon, finds this recipe appeals particularly to men.

For 5 or 6 portions

METRIC	IMPERIAL
1kg best stewing steak	2lb best stewing steak
150g ox kidney	6oz ox kidney
6 shallots or 12 button onions	6 shallots or 12 button onions
25g plain flour	1oz plain flour
1 × 5ml spoon salt	1 level teaspoon salt
Pepper	Pepper
25g lard	1oz lard
½ litre stock, or ½ litre water and 1 beef stock cube	1 pint stock, or 1 pint water and 1 beef stock cube
PASTRY	PASTRY
75g lard	3oz lard
75g margarine	3oz margarine
200g self-raising flour	8oz self-raising flour
1 × 10ml spoon lemon juice	2 teaspoons lemon juice
7 to 8 × 15ml spoons cold water to mix	8 tablespoons cold water to mix
150g mushrooms	6oz mushrooms
Beaten egg or milk to glaze	Beaten egg or milk to glaze

1. Cut steak and kidney into 2cm (1in) cubes, discarding fat and gristle. Peel shallots or onions.
2. Mix 25g (1oz) flour, salt and a shake of pepper together on a plate; coat meat in seasoned flour.
3. Melt 25g (1oz) lard in a large saucepan, add meat and fry quickly, stirring, for 3 minutes. Stir in any remaining seasoned flour, shallots or onions and stock or water and beef stock cube.
4. Bring to boil, stirring. Cover and simmer very slowly for 2 to 3 hours, or until beef is tender; cool quickly. Store in a cold place until ready to make pie.
5. Place lard and margarine on a plate and work together with a palette knife until well mixed. Leave in a cool place until fairly firm, then cut into 2cm (1in) squares.
6. Place flour in a bowl. Add squares of fat, coating each in flour. Add lemon juice and water; mix lightly with a palette knife, then turn out on to a lightly floured board. Form into an oblong, about 38cm by 13cm (15in by 5in), pressing lightly with a rolling pin. Fold dough, bringing top third over centre portion, then cover with lower third and give dough a quarter turn, clockwise, so fold is on the left. Repeat rolling and folding twice more (three rollings in all); wrap in foil and leave in a cold place for several hours, or overnight. (The pastry can be frozen at this stage, if desired: place in a polythene bag and seal tightly.)
7. Prepare a hot oven (220 deg C, 425 deg F, Gas Mark 7). Place cooled meat into a 1 litre (2 pint) pie dish; reserve some of the gravy to serve separately. Wash and quarter mushrooms; add to pie dish.
8. Roll out pastry to an oval, 5cm (2in) larger than top of pie dish. Cut off 1cm (½in) rim from around outside edge of pastry. Brush rim of pie dish with water and press pastry strip in position on rim; brush with water.
9. Lift remaining pastry over rolling pin and place over meat. Press edges together firmly and trim with a knife. Using back of knife, cut edge of pastry, to form flakes. Flute edge in wide flutes by pressing thumb on edge and drawing back of knife towards centre. Make a large hole in centre of pie with point of knife. Roll out pastry trimmings and cut 4 large leaves; brush underside of each leaf with water, arrange on pie. Brush pastry with beaten egg or milk, to glaze.
10. Cook pie just above centre of oven for 30 to 35 minutes, until pastry is golden brown and well risen. Serve pie hot with boiled potatoes, cabbage and reheated gravy from the stewed steak and kidney.

Note: if preferred, the steak and kidney may be cooked in a casserole in a cool oven (170 deg C, 325 deg F, Gas Mark 3) for 2½ to 3 hours.

Savoury Hot Pot

Mrs Christina Mann, from Whitley Bay, finds this recipe very successful with visitors.

For 4 portions

METRIC	IMPERIAL
1kg middle neck of lamb chops	2lb middle neck of lamb chops
1 onion	1 onion
2 carrots	2 carrots
¾kg potatoes	1½lb potatoes
25g lard	½oz lard
1 × 15ml spoon plain flour	1 level tablespoon plain flour
1 × 10ml spoon meat extract	1 rounded teaspoon meat extract
Salt and pepper	Salt and pepper

1. Prepare a moderate oven (180 deg C, 350 deg F, Gas Mark 4).
2. Wipe and trim chops, if necessary. Peel and thinly slice onion, carrots and potatoes.
3. Melt lard in a large frying pan. Add chops and fry quickly, turning once, until browned. Remove from pan and place in a 2 litre (4 pint) casserole.
4. Add onion and carrots to fat in frying pan and fry for 5 minutes; remove from pan and add to casserole. Arrange sliced potatoes, slightly overlapping, on top of casserole.
5. Add flour to fat remaining in pan; mix well. Stir in 250ml (½ pint) water, meat extract and some salt and pepper. Bring to boil, stirring; pour over potatoes and cover with a lid or foil.
6. Bake in centre of oven for 2 hours. Remove lid or foil and continue cooking for a further 15 to 30 minutes, until potatoes are brown. Serve with mashed turnips.

Danish Peasant Girl with Veil

(pictured on page 36)

Jenny Plucknett, Family Circle Home Editor, serves this attractive dessert when she is entertaining, as it can be made in advance.

For 4 portions

METRIC	IMPERIAL
200g fresh white breadcrumbs	8oz fresh white breadcrumbs
100g soft brown sugar (light)	4oz soft brown sugar (light)
75g butter	3oz butter
¾kg cooking apples	1½lb cooking apples
Juice of half a lemon	Juice of half a lemon
50g granulated sugar	2oz granulated sugar
Ground nutmeg	Ground nutmeg
Ground cinnamon	Ground cinnamon
100ml double cream	4 fluid oz double cream
Plain chocolate, grated	Plain chocolate, grated

1. Prepare a moderate grill; remove grill rack and place breadcrumbs in grill pan. Toast breadcrumbs until golden brown.
2. Mix breadcrumbs and brown sugar. Melt butter in a frying pan; add the crumb mixture and fry, stirring occasionally, until crisp and golden brown. Remove from heat and leave to cool.
3. Peel, core and slice apples. Place apples, 1 × 15ml spoon (1 tablespoon) water, lemon juice, granulated sugar and a pinch each of nutmeg and cinnamon in a saucepan. Cover and cook over a moderate heat for about 10 minutes, until apples are soft. Using a wooden spoon, press apples through a sieve into a basin, to make a purée (or liquidise in an electric blender).
4. Place a layer of breadcrumbs in 4 glasses, then a layer of apple; repeat, then top with a layer of breadcrumbs. Place in refrigerator.
5. Place cream in a basin; whisk until thick. Place a spoonful on top of each glass; sprinkle with chocolate.

Chocolate Dairy Crunch

(pictured on page 37)

Mrs Mary McConachie lives on a farm in Nairn, Scotland. Her eight children and her guests always enjoy this delicious dessert.

For 4 portions

METRIC·	IMPERIAL
CRUNCH CASE	CRUNCH CASE
1 (200g) packet gingernut biscuits	1 (7.05oz) packet gingernut biscuits
100g plain chocolate	4oz plain chocolate
75g butter	3oz butter
FILLING	FILLING
150ml double cream	¼ pint double cream
2 × 15ml spoons milk	2 tablespoons milk
1 large (425g) can pear halves	1 large (15oz) can pear halves
DECORATION	DECORATION
Glacé cherries	Glacé cherries

1. Grease a 21.5cm (8½in) pie plate. Place biscuits between 2 sheets of greaseproof paper and crush with a rolling pin.
2. Break up chocolate and place, with butter, in a dry basin over a saucepan of hot, but not boiling, water; stir occasionally until melted. Remove basin from heat and stir in crushed biscuits.
3. Press mixture on base and side of pie plate, to form a case. Leave in refrigerator until firm.
4. Place cream and milk in a basin and whisk until thick. Spread cream in crunch case. Drain pears; cut each pear half in half and arrange pear quarters in a circle on cream. Chop a few glacé cherries and place a little chopped cherry in hollows of pears. Serve cold.

Note: extra pears can be chopped and mixed in with cream or used to make a fruit salad. Fresh fruits, such as strawberries and raspberries, can be used instead.

DANISH PEASANT GIRL WITH VEIL *Recipe on page 35*

CHOCOLATE DAIRY CRUNCH *Recipe on page 35*

Crêpes Margaret

Mrs Peggy Morgan, from Carmarthen in Wales, won first prize with this recipe in one of the Cook of the Year competitions.

For 4 portions

METRIC	IMPERIAL
PANCAKE BATTER	PANCAKE BATTER
25g butter	1oz butter
25g castor sugar	1oz castor sugar
1 egg	1 egg
100g self-raising flour	4oz self-raising flour
125ml milk	¼ pint milk
FILLING	FILLING
1 large (425g) can apricot halves	1 large (15oz) can apricot halves
75g butter	3oz butter
100g icing sugar	4oz icing sugar
Oil or lard for frying	Oil or lard for frying
TOPPING AND DECORATION	TOPPING AND DECORATION
1 × 15ml spoon apricot or peach brandy	1 tablespoon apricot or peach brandy
25g browned, flaked almonds	½oz browned, flaked almonds
6 glacé cherries	6 glacé cherries

1. Cream 25g (1oz) butter and castor sugar together until light. Beat egg and add gradually, beating well after each addition. Fold in flour, alternately with milk; leave for 1 hour.
2. Prepare filling: drain apricots, reserving syrup. Reserve 6 apricot halves for decoration and chop the remainder.
3. Cream butter and icing sugar together. Beat in 1 × 15ml spoon (1 tablespoon) apricot syrup; fold in chopped apricots. Stir 125ml (¼ pint) water into batter.
4. Heat a little oil or lard in a medium-sized frying pan. Pour off excess fat into a small basin, leaving pan lightly greased. Pour about 2 × 15ml spoons (2 tablespoons) of the batter into pan; swirl to coat pan. Cook over a moderate heat, until underside of pancake is golden brown.
5. Slide pancake to side of pan opposite handle; quickly flip over with a palette knife. Cook until other side is golden brown. Invert pancake on to a sheet of greaseproof paper. Use remaining batter to make 7 more pancakes.
6. Prepare a moderately hot oven (200 deg C, 400 deg F, Gas Mark 6). Place about 1 × 10ml spoonful (2 teaspoonsful) of filling in each pancake. Roll up; place in an ovenproof dish.
7. Stir apricot or peach brandy into remaining filling; pour over pancakes. Sprinkle with flaked almonds.
8. Arrange reserved apricot halves, cut sides uppermost, in dish; place a glacé cherry in each.
9. Cook the pancakes on the shelf just above the centre of the oven for 15 minutes and serve hot.

Almond Tutti-Frutti Rice

Mrs Margaret Poppa, from Leeds, cooked this dish in a Cook of the Year competition.

For 4 to 6 portions

METRIC	IMPERIAL
100g pudding rice	4oz pudding rice
½ litre milk	1 pint milk
2 × 15ml spoons castor sugar	1 heaped tablespoon castor sugar
1 × 5ml spoon almond essence	1 teaspoon almond essence
125ml single cream	¼ pint single cream
100g assorted coloured glacé cherries	4oz assorted coloured glacé cherries
125ml double cream	¼ pint double cream
25g blanched almonds	1oz blanched almonds

1. Wash rice thoroughly. Place in a saucepan, with 125ml (¼ pint) water and bring to boil. Simmer very gently for about 7 minutes or until almost dry.
2. Add ½ litre (1 pint) milk and bring to boil. Add sugar and almond essence; simmer for 20 to 25 minutes, until rice is tender. Stir in single cream; leave 5 minutes.
3. Rinse a ¾ litre (1½ pint) mould with water and place 6 cherries around base. Cut rest of cherries into quarters; stir into rice. Pour into mould; leave to cool.
4. Place in refrigerator and leave for 1½ hours. Invert on to a serving plate. Whisk double cream until thick; place in a nylon piping bag, fitted with a large star tube. Pipe stars around top of mould; decorate with almonds.

Baked Stuffed Peaches

Try making this simple dish, the recipe for which comes from Mrs Jill Curtis, of Bury St Edmunds, Suffolk.

For 4 portions

METRIC	IMPERIAL
1 large (822g) can peach halves	1 large (1lb 13oz) can peach halves
25g butter or margarine	1oz butter or margarine
50g desiccated coconut	2oz desiccated coconut
25g demerara sugar	1oz demerara sugar
1 × 2.5 ml spoon cinnamon	½ level teaspoon cinnamon
½ × 2.5ml spoon grated nutmeg	¼ level teaspoon grated nutmeg

1. Prepare a moderate oven (190 deg C, 375 deg F, Gas Mark 5). Butter a shallow, ovenproof dish.
2. Drain peach halves, reserving syrup. Arrange, cut sides uppermost, in dish. Melt butter in a saucepan; add 1 × 15ml spoon (1 tablespoon) peach syrup and other ingredients; mix well. Fill centres of peach halves. Bake in centre of oven for 10 to 15 minutes, until golden.

Bakewell Tart

Mrs Nancy Gammie takes about a dozen guests in her guest house in Penzance, Cornwall, and her recipe for Bakewell Tart is popular with them all.

For 4 or 5 portions

METRIC	IMPERIAL
PASTRY	PASTRY
125g self-raising flour	**4oz self-raising flour**
75g mixed cooking fats	**2oz mixed cooking fats**
Cold water to mix	**Cold water to mix**
FILLING	FILLING
4 × 15ml spoons jam or lemon curd	**2 rounded tablespoons jam or lemon curd**
25g ground rice	**1oz ground rice**
75g ground almonds	**3oz ground almonds**
1 egg	**1 egg**
A few drops almond essence (optional)	**A few drops almond essence (optional)**
50g margarine	**2oz margarine**
50g castor sugar	**2oz castor sugar**
12 blanched almonds (optional)	**12 blanched almonds (optional)**

1. Prepare a moderate oven (190 deg C, 375 deg F, Gas Mark 5). Place an 18cm (7in) fluted flan ring on a baking sheet, or use same-sized sandwich tin.
2. Place flour in a bowl. Add fats, cut into small pieces and rub in with the fingertips until mixture resembles fine breadcrumbs. Add about 1 × 15ml spoon (4 teaspoons) cold water; mix with a fork to a firm dough.
3. Turn out on to a floured board and knead lightly. Roll out to a circle, about 4cm (1½in) larger all around than flan ring. Support pastry on rolling pin and lift on to flan ring. Gently ease pastry into flan ring and press into flutes. Roll off surplus pastry with rolling pin across top of flan ring. Press pastry into flutes again with the fingers; reserve pastry trimmings.
4. Spread jam or lemon curd in flan.
5. Mix ground rice and ground almonds together; beat egg and almond essence, if used, together.
6. Cream margarine and sugar together, until light and fluffy. Add egg gradually, beating well after each addition. Fold in rice and ground almond mixture with a metal spoon.
7. Place almond mixture in flan case and spread over jam; level top with back of spoon.
8. Roll out pastry trimmings to an oblong, about 18cm by 6cm (7in by 2in); cut into 6 thin strips, about 18cm (7in) long. Arrange strips in a lattice pattern over almond mixture; trim ends. If desired, place a blanched almond in each square.
9. Bake in centre of oven for 35 to 45 minutes, until golden brown. Serve warm or cold.

Note: for a more economical recipe, you could replace some of the ground almonds with extra ground rice.

Lemon Apple Pie

Mrs Mary Johnson, from Blackpool, Lancashire, finds this dessert is much appreciated by her guests.

For 6 portions

METRIC	IMPERIAL
FILLING	FILLING
½kg cooking apples	**1lb cooking apples**
Rind of half a lemon	**Rind of half a lemon**
3 cloves	**3 cloves**
4 × 15ml spoons granulated sugar	**2 rounded tablespoons granulated sugar**
SHORTCRUST PASTRY	SHORTCRUST PASTRY
200g plain flour	**8oz plain flour**
1 × 2.5ml spoon salt	**½ level teaspoon salt**
75g lard	**3oz lard**
25g margarine	**1oz margarine**
1 × 15ml spoon castor sugar	**1 level tablespoon castor sugar**
Cold water to mix	**Cold water to mix**
Milk	**Milk**
TOPPING	TOPPING
2 × 10ml spoons granulated sugar	**2 rounded teaspoons granulated sugar**
A pinch of ground cinnamon	**A pinch of ground cinnamon**

1. Peel, core and slice apples; place in a saucepan with the pared rind of lemon (avoid white pith), cloves, sugar and 1 × 15ml spoon (1 tablespoon) water. Cover with a lid and cook over a low heat until apple is pulped; remove from heat, place in a basin and leave overnight or until cold; remove lemon rind and cloves.
2. Prepare a moderately hot oven (200 deg C, 400 deg F, Gas Mark 6). Place flour and salt in a bowl. Add fats, cut into small pieces and rub in with the fingertips until mixture resembles fine breadcrumbs.
3. Dissolve castor sugar in 2 × 15ml spoons (2 tablespoons) cold water; add to bowl and mix to form a really firm dough.
4. Turn out dough on to a floured board and knead lightly; cut into 2 pieces, one slightly larger than the other. Roll out larger piece and line a 20cm (8in) pie plate; roll out other piece for lid. Spread the filling over the pastry.
5. Brush pastry rim of pie with milk and cover with pastry lid. Seal edge firmly, cut up edge with back of a knife, then flute edge with the fingers. Brush pastry top with milk.
6. Mix topping ingredients together in a small basin and sprinkle evenly over pastry. Place pie on a baking sheet and bake in centre of oven for 35 to 40 minutes, until pastry is golden brown. You can serve lemon apple pie warm or cold with custard, ice cream or single cream.

Peacheesy Flan

(pictured right)

Mrs Carol Baxter, from Purley, Surrey, cooked this flan for one of the Cook of the Year competitions.

For 4 portions

METRIC	IMPERIAL
PASTRY	PASTRY
100g plain flour	4oz plain flour
Pinch of salt	Pinch of salt
25g lard	1½oz lard
25g butter	½oz butter
1 × 15ml spoon peach syrup (from can)	1 tablespoon peach syrup (from can)
FILLING	FILLING
1 large (427g) can peach slices	1 large (15oz) can peach slices
1 × 15ml spoon cornflour	1 level tablespoon cornflour
1 × 5ml spoon mixed spice	1 level teaspoon mixed spice
1 × 5ml spoon vanilla essence	1 teaspoon vanilla essence
TOPPING	TOPPING
1 egg	1 egg
75g castor sugar	2½ oz castor sugar
1 × 10ml spoon lemon juice	2 teaspoons lemon juice
2 × 15ml spoons peach syrup	2 tablespoons peach syrup
1 × 15ml spoon soured cream	1 level tablespoon soured cream
50g cream cheese	1½oz cream cheese

PEACHEESY FLAN

1. Prepare a moderately hot oven (200 deg C, 400 deg F, Gas Mark 6). Place a 18cm (7in) fluted flan ring on a baking sheet. (Invert baking sheet, if it has a rim.)
2. Place flour and salt in a bowl. Add fats, cut into small pieces and rub in with the fingertips until mixture resembles fine breadcrumbs. Add 1 × 15ml spoon (1 tablespoon) peach syrup; mix to form a firm dough.
3. Turn out on to a floured board and knead lightly. Roll out pastry to a circle, 4cm (1½in) larger all around than flan ring. Support pastry on rolling pin and lift on to flan ring. Gently ease pastry into flan ring and press into flutes. Roll off surplus pastry with rolling pin across top of flan ring. Press pastry into flutes again with the fingers.
4. Place drained peach slices in a basin; reserve remaining syrup for topping. Stir in cornflour, mixed spice, vanilla essence. Place peach mixture in flan case.
5. Place egg, sugar, lemon juice and 2 × 15ml spoons (2 tablespoons) peach syrup in a small saucepan. Cook over a low heat, stirring, until mixture thickens (do not boil). Remove from heat; beat in soured cream and cream cheese, then pour over peaches.
6. Bake in centre of oven for 10 minutes; reduce oven temperature to moderate (180 deg C, 350 deg F, Gas Mark 4) and cook for a further 25 to 35 minutes, until the topping is golden brown. Serve flan warm or cold.

French Pancakes

This recipe was sent to us from Mrs Gwen Penketh, who lives in Deganwy, Wales.

For 4 portions

METRIC	IMPERIAL
125ml milk	¼ pint milk
50g margarine	2oz margarine
Castor sugar	Castor sugar
2 eggs	2 eggs
50g plain flour	2oz plain flour
4 × 15ml spoons jam	4 level tablespoons jam

1. Prepare a hot oven (220 deg C, 425 deg F, Gas Mark 7). Grease 4 large, 8.5cm (3½in) tartlet tins, 4 old saucers or 4 ovenproof tea plates.
2. Place milk in a small saucepan and heat until just warmed to blood heat.
3. Cream margarine and 50g (2oz) castor sugar together until light and fluffy. Beat eggs together and add to creamed mixture, a little at a time, with 1 × 5ml spoon (1 teaspoon) of the measured flour, beating well after each addition. Stir in the remaining flour and then the warmed milk.
4. Place 2 × 15ml spoons (2 tablespoons) of the mixture in each tartlet tin (cook remaining mixture when the first pancakes are done) or quarter of mixture in each saucer or plate. Bake in centre of oven for 10 to 15 minutes.
5. Sprinkle a little castor sugar on a sheet of greaseproof paper. Warm jam in a small saucepan.
6. When cooked, turn out pancakes on to sugared paper and spread with jam. Fold pancakes in halves and serve immediately.

Note: if desired, all the mixture may be cooked in a 20.5cm (8in) ovenglass pie plate for 20 to 25 minutes.

Pineapple Cheesecake

(pictured below)

The Editor of Pins and Needles *magazine, Joy Mayhew, enjoys cooking as well as sewing and gave us her very special cheesecake recipe.*

For 6 portions

METRIC	IMPERIAL
BASE	**BASE**
125g digestive biscuits	**¼lb digestive biscuits**
50g butter	**1½oz butter**
FILLING	**FILLING**
1 (350g) can pineapple slices	**1 (12oz) can pineapple slices**
200g curd cheese	**½lb curd cheese**
1 egg, beaten	**1 egg, beaten**
1 × 15ml spoon castor sugar	**1 level tablespoon castor sugar**
1 × 2.5ml spoon vanilla essence	**½ teaspoon vanilla essence**
1 × 2.5ml spoon lemon juice	**½ teaspoon lemon juice**
TOPPING	**TOPPING**
150ml soured cream	**¼ pint soured cream**
1 × 15ml spoon castor sugar	**1 level tablespoon castor sugar**
1 × 5ml spoon vanilla essence	**1 teaspoon vanilla essence**

1. Prepare a moderate oven (180 deg C, 350 deg F, Gas Mark 4). Line an 18cm (7in) sandwich tin with foil, so that foil comes about 2.5cm (1in) above rim of tin.

2. Place biscuits between 2 sheets of greaseproof paper; crush finely with a rolling pin.

3. Melt butter in a saucepan; stir in biscuits. place biscuit mixture in prepared tin; press down and level top.

4. Drain pineapple; reserve 1 slice for decoration and chop remainder. Place chopped pineapple, curd cheese, beaten egg, castor sugar, vanilla essence and lemon juice in a bowl; beat together.

5. Place mixture on biscuit base and bake in centre of oven for 25 to 30 minutes, until filling is set. Remove from oven and leave in tin for 1 hour.

6. Mix soured cream, castor sugar and vanilla essence together in a basin. Pour over cheesecake. Return cheesecake to centre of oven and cook for 10 minutes until topping is set. Leave to cool, then chill in refrigerator. Lift cheesecake out of tin and remove foil. Cut the reserved pineapple ring into 8 pieces and place around the edge of the cheesecake.

PINEAPPLE CHEESECAKE

Scandinavian Apple Cake (pictured below)

Mrs Elaine Bastable, from Cheam, finds this dessert a favourite with her four sons and daughter.

For 4 or 5 portions

METRIC	IMPERIAL
½kg cooking apples	1lb cooking apples
2 × 15ml spoons granulated sugar	1 rounded tablespoon granulated sugar
½ × 2.5ml spoon cinnamon	¼ level teaspoon ground cinnamon
25g sultanas	1oz sultanas
250g Madeira cake	10oz Madeira cake
50g butter	2oz butter
Finely grated rind of 1 lemon	Finely grated rind of 1 lemon
1 × 15ml spoon lemon juice	1 tablespoon lemon juice
Icing sugar to decorate	Icing sugar to decorate

1. Prepare a moderate oven (190 deg C, 375 deg F, Gas Mark 5). Thoroughly butter a deep, round 15cm (6in) loose-based cake tin.

2. Peel, core and slice apples. Place in a saucepan, with 1 × 15ml spoon (1 tablespoon) water and sugar. Cook over a low heat, stirring continuously, until soft and thick. Stir in cinnamon and sultanas; leave to cool.

3. Crumble cake. Melt butter in a saucepan; leave to cool; add lemon rind, juice and cake crumbs.

4. Divide crumb mixture into 3. Press one third into base of tin; spread with half the apple; repeat layers. Press remaining crumbs firmly on top.

5. Place on a baking sheet in centre of oven and cook for 20 to 30 minutes, until golden. Cool slightly, remove from tin and place on a serving dish.

6. To decorate: cut 4 strips of card, each measuring 16.5cm by 2cm (6½in by ¾in). Lay strips across tops of cake in the same direction. Dredge icing sugar over. Remove strips carefully and replace in the opposite direction. Dredge with icing sugar to give the squared effect. Remove the strips of card. Serve apple cake warm or cold with cream, custard or ice cream.

SCANDINAVIAN APPLE CAKE

Pineapple Meringue Tarts

Mrs Andrea Hutchinson, from Ipswich in Suffolk, entered one of the Cook of the Year competitions.

Makes 4

METRIC	IMPERIAL
150g plain flour	5oz plain flour
Pinch of salt	Pinch of salt
50g lard	1½oz lard
50g margarine	1½oz margarine
1 × 10ml spoon icing sugar	1 rounded teaspoon icing sugar
1 egg yolk	1 egg yolk
Cold water to mix	Cold water to mix
FILLING	FILLING
1 (226g) can pineapple pieces	1 (8oz) can pineapple pieces
25g butter	½oz butter
25g flour	½oz flour
1 egg yolk	1 egg yolk
2 egg whites	2 egg whites
100g castor sugar	4oz castor sugar

1. Prepare a moderately hot oven (200 deg C, 400 deg F, Gas Mark 6). Place 4, 11.25cm (4½in) foil baking cases on a baking sheet.

2. Sift flour and salt into a bowl. Add fats, cut into small pieces and rub in with the fingertips until mixture resembles fine breadcrumbs. Mix in icing sugar. Beat egg yolk and 1 × 15ml spoon (1 tablespoon) water together. Add to pastry and mix with a fork to form a firm dough.

3. Turn out on to a floured board and knead lightly. Cut into 4 and roll each piece to a 15cm (6in) circle. Press circles gently into baking cases; trim and flute edges. Line cases with greaseproof paper; fill with baking beans or rice.

4. Place cases on a baking sheet and bake in centre of oven for 10 minutes. Remove paper and beans or rice and return cases to oven; leave to cook for a further 4 to 6 minutes, until pastry is golden brown. Reduce oven temperature to cool (150 deg C, 300 deg F, Gas Mark 2).

5. Drain syrup from pineapple into a measuring jug, and make up to 150ml (¼ pint) with water. Cut each pineapple piece in half.

6. Melt butter in a saucepan, stir in flour and cook gently, without browning, for 1 minute. Add pineapple syrup and bring to boil, stirring continuously; cook for 1 minute. Remove from heat, beat in egg yolk and pineapple; divide between pastry cases.

7. Place egg whites in a clean, grease-free basin and whisk until stiff, but not dry. Reserve 1 × 5ml spoon (1 teaspoon) castor sugar, then whisk in half of remainder; fold in remaining half, cutting through mixture with a metal spoon. Spread meringue over filling in each case; sprinkle with reserved castor sugar. Return to oven and cook for a further 30 minutes, until meringue is golden brown. Remove from foil cases and serve warm or cold.

Croft House Flan

Mrs Mona Hutton, from Inverness in Scotland, enjoys making this delicious flan for her family, who certainly enjoy eating it.

For 6 to 8 portions

METRIC	IMPERIAL
SHORTCRUST PASTRY	SHORTCRUST PASTRY
150g plain flour	6oz plain flour
½ × 2.5ml spoon salt	¼ level teaspoon salt
75g mixed cooking fats	3oz mixed cooking fats
Cold water to mix	Cold water to mix
FILLING	FILLING
¼kg cooking apples	½lb cooking apples
50g sultanas	2oz sultanas
2 eggs	2 eggs
250g Crowdie or cottage cheese	½lb Crowdie or cottage cheese
1 × 15ml spoon cornflour	1 level tablespoon cornflour
25g castor sugar	1oz castor sugar
1 × 15ml spoon milk	1 tablespoon milk

1. Prepare a moderate oven (190 deg C, 375 deg F, Gas Mark 5). Place a 20cm (8in) fluted flan ring on a baking sheet.

2. Place flour and salt in a bowl. Add fats, cut into small pieces and rub in with the fingertips until mixture resembles fine breadcrumbs. Add about 2 × 10ml spoons (1½ tablespoons) water and mix with a fork to form a firm dough.

3. Turn out on to a floured board and knead lightly. Roll out pastry to a circle, 4cm (1½in) larger all around than flan ring. Support pastry on rolling pin and lift on to flan ring. Gently ease pastry into flan ring and press into flutes. Roll off surplus pastry with a rolling pin across the top of the flan ring. Press pastry into the flutes again with the fingers.

4. Peel, core and slice apples. Stew in a covered saucepan, with 1 × 15ml spoon (1 tablespoon) water, until tender. Beat until smooth. Leave to cool.

5. Spread the apple mixture in pastry case and cover with a sprinkling of sultanas.

6. Separate eggs and place egg whites in a clean, grease-free bowl. Sieve cheese into a basin; add egg yolks, cornflour, sugar and milk and mix well. Whisk egg whites until stiff, but not dry, and fold into cheese mixture. Pile into pastry case.

7. Bake in centre of oven for 25 minutes. Remove flan ring and bake for a further 10 to 15 minutes, until golden brown. Place the flan on a wire rack and leave until cold.

*Catering for sharp
home-from-school appetites
isn't always easy. But these quick savoury recipes you have
sent to us are ideal – simple to make, tasty, nutritious and economical*

Sausage and Leek Pie

*Follow this recipe, which comes from Mrs Betty Kerr of
Brockweir in Gloucestershire – it's her family's favourite.*

For 4 to 6 portions

METRIC	IMPERIAL
½kg leeks	1lb leeks
2 eggs	2 eggs
Salt and pepper	Salt and pepper
SHORTCRUST	SHORTCRUST
PASTRY	PASTRY
300g plain flour	¾lb plain flour
1 × 5ml spoon salt	1 level teaspoon salt
75g margarine	3oz margarine
75g lard	3oz lard
Cold water to mix	Cold water to mix
300g pork sausagemeat	¾lb pork sausagemeat

1. Prepare a moderately hot oven (200 deg C, 400 deg F, Gas Mark 6).
2. Trim roots, tops and tough outside leaves from leeks. Cut leeks half way through lengthwise, then open out and wash thoroughly, to remove any soil. Cut into 1cm (½in) rings. Beat eggs in a bowl with a little salt and pepper.
3. Place flour and salt in a bowl. Add fats, cut into small pieces, and rub in with the fingertips until mixture resembles fine breadcrumbs. Add about 3 × 15ml spoons (3 tablespoons) of water and mix to form a firm dough.
4. Turn out on to a floured board and knead lightly. Roll out half the pastry and line an 18cm (7in) sandwich tin. Brush edges with water.
5. Place half the leeks in tin; cover with pieces of sausagemeat and top with remaining leeks. Pour beaten egg over, reserving 1 × 10ml spoon (2 teaspoons) for brushing pastry. Roll out remaining pastry and cover pie; press edges together and trim. Cut up edges with the back of a knife to form flakes and flute; brush pie with egg. Make a small hole in centre of pie. Roll out trimmings and cut out leaves; arrange on pie and brush with egg.
6. Bake just above centre of oven for 15 minutes, then reduce oven temperature to cool (170 deg C, 325 deg F, Gas Mark 3) and bake for 1 to 1¼ hours. Serve cold.

Highland Broth

*Mrs Mary McConachie and her family, from Nairn in
Scotland, find this dish very nourishing after long walks.*

For 8 to 10 portions

METRIC	IMPERIAL
1 beef marrow bone	1 beef marrow bone
6 × 15ml spoons broth or soup mix (see note)	3 rounded tablespoons broth or soup mix (see note)
Boiling water	Boiling water
½ × 2.5ml spoon bicarbonate of soda	¼ level teaspoon bicarbonate of soda
Salt and pepper	Salt and pepper
1 large onion	1 large onion
1 large leek	1 large leek
150g piece turnip	6oz piece turnip
1 large carrot	1 large carrot
4 leaves green cabbage	4 leaves green cabbage
1 × 15ml spoon chopped parsley	1 level tablespoon chopped parsley

1. Ask butcher to chop marrow bone. Place broth or soup mix in a bowl and cover with boiling water. Add bicarbonate of soda and leave overnight; drain.
2. Place marrow bone in a large saucepan. Add 3 litres (6 pints) cold water, broth or soup mix, 1 × 15ml spoon (3 level teaspoons) salt and a good shake of pepper. Bring to boil and skim. Return to boil, cover and simmer for about 2 hours, until broth or soup mix is tender. Remove marrow bone and skim stock thoroughly.
3. Peel and finely chop onion. Trim off root and any tough outside leaves from leek. Cut leek half way through lengthwise; open out and wash thoroughly, to remove any soil; cut into rings. Peel turnip and carrot; cut into small dice.
4. Add vegetables to stock. Bring to boil, cover and simmer for 20 minutes until vegetables are just tender. Wash cabbage leaves and shred finely; add to saucepan. Cook for a further 8 to 10 minutes, until tender.
5. Taste and season with salt and pepper, if necessary. Sprinkle broth with chopped parsley. Serve hot, with crusty bread.
Note: if you are unable to obtain broth or soup mix, replace with pearl barley, split peas and lentils, mixed. If desired, a beef stock cube may be added to the broth.

Savoury Rarebit

(pictured right)

Mrs Molly Tandisides, one of our readers from Doncaster, sent us this recipe, which we're sure you'll want to try.

For 2 portions

METRIC	IMPERIAL
4 to 6 rashers streaky bacon	4 to 6 rashers streaky bacon
4 large tomatoes	4 large tomatoes
Oil	Oil
100g Cheddar cheese	4oz Cheddar cheese
1 egg	1 egg
25g butter	1oz butter
1 × 15ml spoon tomato ketchup	1 level tablespoon tomato ketchup
1 × 15ml spoon brown sauce	1 level tablespoon brown sauce
1 × 2.5ml spoon salt	½ level teaspoon salt
Pepper	Pepper
4 rounds white or wholemeal bread	4 rounds white or wholemeal bread
Watercress to garnish	Watercress to garnish

SAVOURY RAREBIT

1. Remove rack from grill pan and prepare a moderate grill.

2. Remove rind and bone from bacon; place bacon on a board and flatten with back of knife. Cut rashers in halves and roll up each piece loosely. Slice tomatoes thickly. Arrange bacon rolls and tomato slices in grill pan; brush tomatoes with a little oil. Grill for 6 minutes, turning once.

3. Grate cheese and beat egg. Melt butter in a saucepan, add tomato ketchup, brown sauce, salt and a shake of pepper. Remove from heat and stir in cheese and egg.

4. Arrange rounds of bread on grill rack and return to grill pan over bacon and tomatoes. Toast one side of bread rounds, then turn over and spread with cheese mixture. Grill until golden brown and bubbling.

5. Sandwich 2 rounds together, cheese sides uppermost, with tomato slices. Top with the bacon rolls and garnish with the watercress. Serve the rarebit immediately.

Popovers

Mrs Elaine Bastable, from Southfields, Wimbledon, cooks these when entertaining her son's friends to tea.

For 6 portions

METRIC	IMPERIAL
25g dripping or cooking fat	1oz dripping or cooking fat
100g plain flour	4oz plain flour
1 × 2.5ml spoon mixed dried herbs	½ level teaspoon mixed dried herbs
1 egg	1 egg
Scant 250ml milk and water, mixed	Scant ½ pint milk and water, mixed
75g lean streaky bacon	3oz lean streaky bacon
50g to 75g cheese, grated	2oz to 3oz cheese, grated

1. Prepare a hot oven (230 deg C, 450 deg F, Gas Mark 8). Divide dripping or fat between 18 small bun tins; place in oven to heat.

2. Place flour and mixed dried herbs in a bowl. Make a well in centre of flour and add egg. Stir in half the milk mixture gradually; mix well and beat until smooth. Add remaining liquid; pour into a jug. Remove rind and bone from bacon; cut bacon into small pieces.

3. Divide bacon between bun tins and return tins to oven for 2 to 3 minutes, until bacon sizzles. Pour batter into tins and bake in top position of oven for 15 to 20 minutes, until batter is risen and golden brown.

4. Remove from oven and quickly place 1 × 5ml spoon (1 teaspoon) of grated cheese into each popover. Return to oven for 1 to 2 minutes, to melt cheese. Serve popovers hot, alone, or with baked beans, or fried eggs.

45

Liver and Bacon Risotto

Mrs Helen Crombie, from Edinburgh, cooked this dish in one of our Cook of the Year competitions.

For 6 portions

METRIC	IMPERIAL
RISOTTO	RISOTTO
2 chicken stock cubes	2 chicken stock cubes
½ litre boiling water	1 pint boiling water
1 small onion	1 small onion
Half a medium-sized cooking apple	Half a medium-sized cooking apple
150g long-grain rice	6oz long-grain rice
Chopped parsley	Chopped parsley
1 small (226g) can tomatoes	1 small (8oz) can tomatoes
25g butter	1oz butter
½ × 2.5ml spoon nutmeg	¼ level teaspoon nutmeg
1 × 5ml spoon curry powder	1 level teaspoon curry powder
1 × 2.5ml spoon salt	½ level teaspoon salt
Pepper	Pepper
4 rashers streaky bacon	4 rashers streaky bacon
SAUCE	SAUCE
¼kg chicken livers	½lb chicken livers
2 × 15ml spoons plain flour	2 level tablespoons plain flour
Salt and pepper	Salt and pepper
1 small onion	1 small onion
50g butter	2oz butter
2 medium-sized tomatoes	2 medium-sized tomatoes

1. Prepare a moderate oven (180 deg C, 350 deg F, Gas Mark 4).
2. To make risotto: dissolve stock cubes in boiling water. Peel and chop small onion. Peel, core and chop apple.
3. Place rice and 375ml (¾ pint) of stock in a saucepan; reserve remaining stock for sauce. Bring to boil; stir in chopped onion, apple, 2 × 15ml spoons (2 level tablespoons) chopped parsley, contents of can of tomatoes, 25g (1oz) butter, nutmeg, curry powder, salt and shake of pepper. Cover and simmer for 10 minutes.
4. Place rice mixture in a 1 litre (2 pint) casserole. Cover and cook in centre of oven for 15 minutes, until stock has been absorbed and rice is cooked.
5. Remove rind and bone from bacon; place bacon on a board and flatten with back of knife. Cut rashers in halves and roll up each piece loosely. Place bacon rolls on an ovenproof plate; cook in centre of oven for 10 minutes.
6. To make sauce: cut chicken livers into small pieces. Mix flour, a little salt and a shake of pepper together on a plate; toss chicken livers in seasoned flour, to coat. Peel onion; slice one half and chop remainder.
7. Melt 50g (2oz) butter in a frying pan. Fry onion rings for 2 to 3 minutes, until browned. Remove from frying pan; keep warm. Add chopped onion to fat remaining in pan and cook for 2 to 3 minutes. Add chicken livers and cook for 2 minutes, turning occasionally. Stir in any remaining seasoned flour and reserved stock. Bring to boil, stirring, and cook for 2 minutes.
8. Place tomatoes in a basin and cover with boiling water. Leave for 1 minute; drain, then peel and slice. Place on an ovenproof plate and place in oven to heat through.
9. To serve: place rice on a warmed oblong serving dish. Reheat liver mixture and place in centre of rice. Place slices of tomato, overlapping, from each corner of dish to centre. Arrange bacon rolls between tomatoes and place fried onion rings in centre. Sprinkle some chopped parsley over tomatoes. Serve with a green salad.

Scotch Kedgeree

Mrs Seona Laird, from Kilmacolm in Renfrewshire, finds this a most popular high-tea dish.

For 4 portions

METRIC	IMPERIAL
200g long-grain rice	8oz long-grain rice
1 egg	1 egg
½kg smoked haddock fillet	1lb smoked haddock fillet
75g butter or margarine	3oz butter or margarine
1 small lemon	1 small lemon
½ × 2.5ml spoon nutmeg	¼ level teaspoon nutmeg
Salt and pepper	Salt and pepper
1 × 10ml spoon chopped parsley	1 rounded teaspoon chopped parsley

1. Cook rice in a large saucepan of boiling, salted water for about 12 minutes. Test by pressing a grain between thumb and finger. Drain in a sieve or colander and rinse with boiling water.
2. Hard boil egg for 10 minutes, crack and leave to cool in cold water. Shell and dry on kitchen paper; cut into quarters.
3. Remove skin and bones from fish; cut fish into neat pieces.
4. Melt butter or margarine in a frying pan or saucepan. Add fish; cook for 3 to 4 minutes, turning occasionally. Cut 4 slices from lemon and squeeze juice from remainder.
5. Stir rice, lemon juice and nutmeg into pan. Taste and season with salt and pepper.
6. Pile on to a warmed serving dish. Sprinkle with parsley and garnish with egg quarters and lemon slices.

Tasmanian Tuna Pie
(pictured above)

Mr Charles Calvert, who comes from Birmingham, was a finalist in one of our Cook of the Year competitions, where he cooked this dish.

For 6 portions

METRIC	IMPERIAL
RICE BORDER	**RICE BORDER**
1 medium-sized onion	**1 medium-sized onion**
150g long-grain rice	**6oz long-grain rice**
1 × 5ml spoon turmeric	**1 level teaspoon turmeric**
1 chicken stock cube	**1 chicken stock cube**
1 × 5ml spoon salt	**1 level teaspoon salt**
Pepper	**Pepper**
1 × 10ml spoon oil	**2 teaspoons oil**
1 egg	**1 egg**
FILLING	**FILLING**
1 (198g) can tuna	**1 (7oz) can tuna**
50g strong-flavoured Cheddar cheese	**2oz strong-flavoured Cheddar cheese**
2 eggs	**2 eggs**
1 small can evaporated milk	**1 small can evaporated milk**
1 chicken stock cube	**1 chicken stock cube**
GARNISH	**GARNISH**
Tomato slices	**Tomato slices**
Sprigs of parsley	**Sprigs of parsley**

1. Prepare a moderate oven (180 deg C, 350 deg F, Gas Mark 4). Lightly grease a shallow 23cm (9in) ovenproof dish.

2. Peel and finely chop onion; reserve. Measure 375ml (¾ pint) water into a medium-sized saucepan. Bring to boil; add rice, turmeric, crumbled stock cube, salt, a shake of pepper and oil. Bring to boil, stirring; reduce heat, cover with a lid and simmer for 15 minutes, until rice has absorbed all the liquid. Stir in one quarter of reserved onion.

3. Turn out rice into a mixing bowl; fluff up with a fork and leave until cooled. Lightly beat egg; add to rice and stir in carefully. Place rice in greased dish and press over base and up sides, to form a rice shell.

4. Drain oil from tuna; flake fish and arrange in base of rice shell. Finely grate cheese. Place eggs in a bowl; beat lightly. Stir in evaporated milk, grated cheese, remaining onion and crumbled stock cube. Pour mixture carefully over tuna.

5. Bake in centre of oven for 30 to 40 minutes, until a knife inserted into centre comes out cleanly. Serve the tuna pie either hot or cold and garnished with the tomato slices, cut into quarters, and the sprigs of parsley.

Gougère with Kidney and Bacon Salpicon

(pictured below)

Mrs Gillian Neale, from King's Langley in Hertfordshire, won first prize with this dish in one of our Cook of the Year competitions.

For 4 portions

METRIC	IMPERIAL
GOUGERE	GOUGERE
50g Cheddar cheese	2oz Cheddar cheese
50g butter	2oz butter
75g plain flour	2½oz plain flour
2 eggs	2 eggs
1 × 2.5ml spoon salt	½ level teaspoon salt
Pepper	Pepper
1 × 2.5ml spoon dry mustard	½ level teaspoon dry mustard

GOUGERE WITH KIDNEY AND BACON SALPICON

TOPPING
25g fresh white
    breadcrumbs
25g Cheddar cheese

SALPICON
1 medium-sized onion
75g mushrooms
2 tomatoes from a can
3 lambs' kidneys
2 rashers streaky bacon
50g butter
25g plain flour
1 beef stock cube
125ml boiling water
1 × 10ml spoon tomato
    purée
1 × 2.5ml spoon salt
Pepper
1 × 5ml spoon dried
    basil

TOPPING
1oz fresh white
    breadcrumbs
1oz Cheddar cheese

SALPICON
1 medium-sized onion
3oz mushrooms
2 tomatoes from a can
3 lambs' kidneys
2 rashers streaky bacon
1½oz butter
1oz plain flour
1 beef stock cube
¼ pint boiling water
1 rounded teaspoon
    tomato purée
½ level teaspoon salt
Pepper
1 level teaspoon dried
    basil

1. Prepare a moderately hot oven (200 deg C, 400 deg F, Gas Mark 6).
2. To make gougère: cut 50g (2oz) cheese into small dice. Grease a 23cm (9in) fluted gougère dish, or a shallow oval ovenproof dish. Place 125ml (¼ pint) water and 50g (2oz) butter in a small saucepan; bring to boil. Remove from heat and stir in 75g (2½oz) flour; beat well, until mixture leaves side of pan.
3. If mixture does not leave side of pan, return saucepan to a low heat and beat continuously, until mixture leaves side of pan. Leave to cool slightly.
4. Whisk eggs and beat into mixture, a little at a time, beating well after each addition. Stir in cheese, salt, a shake of pepper and mustard; mix well. Spoon mixture around edge of gougère dish, to form a border.
5. To make topping: spread breadcrumbs on a baking sheet and bake just above centre of oven for 5 minutes, until lightly browned. Grate 25g (1oz) cheese and reserve.
6. To make salpicon: peel and finely chop onion. Wash and slice mushrooms. Chop tomatoes coarsely. Cut kidneys in halves and remove skin and core; cut each half into 6. Remove rind and bone from bacon, then chop bacon finely.
7. Melt 50g (1½oz) butter in a medium-sized saucepan; add kidney and bacon and fry quickly for 5 minutes. Remove kidney and bacon from pan with a draining spoon; place on a plate. Add onion to pan and fry gently, without browning, for 5 minutes; add mushrooms and fry for a further 2 minutes. Stir in 25g (1oz) flour; cook, without browning, for 2 minutes. Dissolve stock cube in boiling water; add to pan. Bring to boil, stirring. Remove from heat, stir in tomato purée, salt, a shake of pepper, basil, tomatoes, kidneys and bacon. Pour salpicon into centre of gougère dish.
8. Mix together browned breadcrumbs and cheese for topping and sprinkle over. Bake in centre of oven for 30 to 40 minutes, until gougère is risen and golden brown. Serve with green salad and jacket potatoes, topped with soured cream and chives.

Curried Mince

Mrs Christina Mann, from Whitley Bay, finds this recipe a very popular one with her guests.

For 4 portions

METRIC	IMPERIAL
1 large onion	1 large onion
25g dripping	½oz dripping
½kg minced beef	1lb minced beef
2 × 15ml spoons curry powder	1 rounded tablespoon curry powder
1 × 15ml spoon plain flour	1 level tablespoon plain flour
250ml beef stock or water	½ pint beef stock or water
Half a 375g can pineapple tid-bits	Half a 13oz can pineapple tid-bits
1 × 10ml spoon black treacle	1 rounded teaspoon black treacle
1 × 15ml spoon chutney	1 level tablespoon chutney
Salt and pepper	Salt and pepper
200g long-grain rice	8oz long-grain rice

GARNISH	GARNISH
2 tomatoes	2 tomatoes
Parsley	Parsley

1. Peel and slice onion. Melt dripping in a saucepan, add onion and fry for 3 to 4 minutes, until golden brown. Add minced beef and curry powder; cook, stirring occasionally, for about 5 minutes. Add flour and cook for 1 minute.
2. Stir in stock or water. Add fruit and syrup from can of pineapple, treacle, chutney, some salt and a shake of pepper. Bring to boil; cover and simmer for 1 hour, stirring occasionally.
3. Cook rice in a large saucepan of boiling, salted water for about 12 minutes. Test by pressing a grain between thumb and finger. Drain in a sieve or colander and rinse with boiling water.
4. Arrange rice around the edge of a large, warmed serving dish. Pour curry in centre of rice. Slice tomatoes and arrange along centre of curry. Garnish with parsley.

Apple Flan

(pictured below)

Yvonne Lyddon, Fashion Editor of Family Circle, provides us with this tasty recipe.

For 4 portions

METRIC	IMPERIAL
PASTRY	PASTRY
125g plain flour	**5oz plain flour**
75g butter	**3oz butter**
Cold water to mix	**Cold water to mix**
FILLING	FILLING
¾kg medium-sized cooking apples	**1½lb medium-sized cooking apples**
1 × 15ml spoon lemon juice	**1 tablespoon lemon juice**
Granulated sugar	**Granulated sugar**
Knob of butter	**Knob of butter**
GLAZE	GLAZE
1 × 5ml spoon arrowroot or cornflour	**1 level teaspoon arrowroot or cornflour**
2 × 15ml spoons apricot jam	**1 rounded tablespoon apricot jam**
1 × 10ml spoon lemon juice	**2 teaspoons lemon juice**

1. Prepare a moderate oven (190 deg C, 375 deg F, Gas Mark 5). Place an 18cm (7in) flan ring on a baking sheet. (Invert baking sheet, if it has a rim.)
2. Place flour in a bowl. Add butter, cut into small pieces and rub in with the fingertips until mixture resembles fine breadcrumbs. Add about 1 × 15ml spoon (1 tablespoon) water and mix to form a firm dough.
3. Turn out on to a floured board and knead lightly. Roll out pastry to a circle, 4cm (1½in) larger all around than flan ring. Roll pastry around rolling pin and lift on to flan ring. Gently ease pastry into flan ring with the fingers. Roll off surplus pastry with rolling pin across top of flan ring. Press pastry into flan ring again with the fingers.
4. Peel, core and slice apples. Place 1 sliced apple in a basin; add 1 × 15ml spoon (1 tablespoon) lemon juice and turn gently, to coat apple in juice; reserve for topping. Place remaining apples, with 2 × 15ml spoons (2 tablespoons) water, in a medium-sized saucepan. Cover and cook over a moderate heat for about 10 minutes, until apples are soft. Add about 50g (2oz) granulated sugar; taste and add more sugar, if desired. Add a knob of butter; beat together. Pour apples into flan case. Place reserved apple slices, overlapping, in 2 circles on apple mixture. Sprinkle with a little sugar.
5. Cook just above centre of oven for 25 to 30 minutes.
6. Blend arrowroot or cornflour with 1 × 10ml spoon (2 teaspoons) water in a saucepan. Add jam, 1 × 10ml spoon (2 teaspoons) lemon juice and 2 × 15ml spoons (2 tablespoons) water. Bring to boil, stirring, and cook for 1 minute; pour over apples in flan case. Serve apple flan hot or cold with cream, custard or ice cream.

APPLE FLAN

Sunflower Gâteau

Mrs Irene Moody was a finalist in one of our Cook of the Year competitions. She comes from Market Harborough in Leicestershire.

METRIC	IMPERIAL
MERINGUES	**MERINGUES**
1 egg white	**1 egg white**
50g castor sugar	**2oz castor sugar**
CAKE	**CAKE**
25g plain chocolate	**1oz plain chocolate**
3 × 15ml spoons boiling water	**3 tablespoons boiling water**
100g plain flour	**3½oz plain flour**
1 × 2.5ml spoon baking powder	**½ level teaspoon baking powder**
1 × 2.5ml spoon bicarbonate of soda	**½ level teaspoon bicarbonate of soda**
50g butter	**2oz butter**
75g soft brown sugar (light)	**2½oz soft brown sugar (light)**
1 egg	**1 egg**
FILLING AND TOPPING	**FILLING AND TOPPING**
1 × 5ml spoon instant coffee	**1 level teaspoon instant coffee**
50g plain chocolate	**1½oz plain chocolate**
1 × 10ml spoon rum	**1 dessertspoon rum**
125ml double cream	**4 fluid oz double cream**
1 (312g) can mandarin oranges	**1 (11oz) can mandarin oranges**

1. Prepare a moderate oven (180 deg C, 350 deg F, Gas Mark 4). Brush a baking sheet with oil or melted fat and line with greaseproof paper; grease paper. Brush an 18cm (7in) sandwich tin with melted fat or oil. Line base with a circle of greaseproof paper; grease paper.
2. To make meringues: place egg white in a clean, grease-free bowl; whisk until stiff, but not dry. Whisk in half the castor sugar; fold in remainder with a metal spoon. Place mixture in a large nylon piping bag fitted with a large star tube. Pipe stars of meringue on to lined baking sheet. Cook in coolest part of oven for 1 to 1½ hours, until crisp, dry and pale golden brown. If meringues brown before they become dry and crisp, remove from oven and leave to dry out in warming drawer of cooker, if possible.
3. To make cake: chop 25g (1oz) chocolate and place in a small basin; add boiling water and stir until chocolate has melted. Sift flour, baking powder and bicarbonate of soda together.
4. Cream butter and brown sugar together until light and fluffy. Beat egg and add gradually, beating well after each addition. Fold in flour, alternately with melted chocolate mixture. Turn out into prepared tin; level top. Bake just above centre of oven for 25 to 40 minutes.

Test by pressing with the fingers. If cooked, cake should spring back and have begun to shrink from side of tin. Turn out, remove paper and leave to cool on a wire rack.
5. To make filling: place instant coffee in a small saucepan, add 1 × 15ml spoon (1 tablespoon) water and stir over a low heat until coffee has dissolved. Chop 50g (1½oz) chocolate; add to saucepan. Stir over a very low heat, until chocolate has melted. Remove from heat; leave to cool. Stir in rum; leave to cool.
6. Whip cream until just stiff. Reserve half the cream; gradually whisk chocolate mixture into remaining cream. Drain mandarin oranges.
7. Split cake in half horizontally. Spread filling on bottom half of cake; replace top. Place cake on a plate. Spread about two thirds of reserved cream over top of cake. Arrange mandarin oranges on top of cake, radiating out from centre.
8. Arrange meringues around side of cake, securing them with a little of the reserved cream. Spoon remaining cream in centre of gâteau.
Note: meringues may be made up to 1 week in advance. If cooking them alone in the oven, set oven to coolest setting and place meringues on shelf in lowest position in oven. Dry out meringues for about 2 hours or until crisp and dry and easily removed from the paper.

Strawberry Fluff

Mrs Patricia Hood, a Reader Club member, developed this recipe one day, when she wanted to make a mousse from her home-grown strawberries, but had no cream in the house.

For 4 portions

METRIC	IMPERIAL
¼kg fresh or frozen strawberries	**½lb fresh or frozen strawberries**
150ml natural yoghourt	**5 fluid oz natural yoghourt**
1 × 10ml spoon gelatine	**2 level teaspoons gelatine**
1 egg white	**1 egg white**

1. Wash strawberries; reserve 4 for decoration and hull remainder. Using a wooden spoon, press strawberries through a nylon sieve into a basin, to make a purée. Beat in yoghourt or liquidise strawberries with yoghourt in an electric blender; pour into a basin.
2. Place 4 × 15ml spoons (4 tablespoons) water in a small basin; add gelatine. Place basin in a saucepan of hot water over a moderate heat and stir until gelatine has dissolved. Stir into strawberry mixture; leave in a cool place until mixture starts to thicken.
3. Place egg white in a clean, grease-free basin and whisk until stiff, but not dry. Fold into strawberry mixture and pour into 4 individual glass dishes. Place in refrigerator and leave for 1 hour or until set. Decorate with reserved strawberries.
Note: add sugar to strawberry purée, if desired.

Minstrel Tart

Mrs Mollie Handisides, from Doncaster, sent us this recipe, which her children love.

For 4 to 6 portions

METRIC
½kg cooking apples
4 × 15ml spoons
  sugar

SHORTCRUST
PASTRY
250g plain flour
1 × 5ml spoon salt
125g mixed cooking fats
Cold water to mix

4 × 15ml spoons
  mincemeat

IMPERIAL
1lb cooking apples
2 heaped tablespoons
  sugar

SHORTCRUST
PASTRY
8oz plain flour
1 level teaspoon salt
4oz mixed cooking fats
Cold water to mix

2 heaped tablespoons
  mincemeat

1. Prepare a hot oven (220 deg C, 425 deg F, Gas Mark 7).

2. Peel, core and thinly slice apples. Cover the bottom of a large saucepan with water, add sugar and stir over a moderate heat, until sugar has dissolved. Add apples and bring to boil. Cook for 1 to 2 minutes, until apples are tender, but not pulped. Place saucepan in a bowl of cold water to cool.

3. Place flour and salt in a bowl. Add fats, cut into small pieces and rub in with the fingertips until mixture resembles fine breadcrumbs. Add about 2 × 15ml spoons (2 tablespoons) cold water and mix to form a firm dough.

4. Turn out on to a floured board and knead lightly. Roll out three quarters of the pastry and line a 25cm (10in) ovenglass plate. Trim edges and re-roll with remaining pastry to a 25cm by 12cm (10in by 6in) oblong. Cut into 12, 25cm by 1cm (10in by ½in) strips.

5. Drain apples and spread over pastry to within 1cm (½in) of edge. Spread mincemeat, a little at a time, in a thin layer over centre. Dampen edges of pastry.

6. Twist pastry strips and arrange in a lattice over filling. Trim ends, press strips on to pastry; flute edge.

7. Place on a baking sheet and cook in top position of oven for 15 to 25 minutes, until pastry is golden brown. Serve hot or cold, with custard or cream.

BITTER-SWEET FLAN

Bitter-sweet Flan

(pictured below left)

Mrs Grace Brady, from Nantwich in Cheshire, was a finalist in one of our Cook of the Year competitions, with this recipe.

For 4 to 6 portions

METRIC	IMPERIAL
PASTRY	PASTRY
1 small egg	1 small egg
25g castor sugar	1oz castor sugar
200g plain flour	8oz plain flour
50g margarine	2oz margarine
50g lard	2oz lard
LEMON FILLING	LEMON FILLING
1 lemon	1 lemon
1 × 15ml spoon cornflour	1 level tablespoon cornflour
50g castor sugar	2oz castor sugar
1 egg yolk	1 egg yolk
CHOCOLATE FILLING	CHOCOLATE FILLING
50g plain chocolate	2oz plain chocolate
25g cornflour	1oz cornflour
250ml milk	½ pint milk
1 × 15ml spoon castor sugar	1 level tablespoon castor sugar
DECORATION	DECORATION
1 small (48g) packet dessert topping mix	1 small (1oz 11dr) packet dessert topping mix
Milk	Milk
Toasted, shredded almonds	Toasted, shredded almonds

1. Prepare a moderate oven (190 deg C, 375 deg F, Gas Mark 5). Place a 20cm (8in) fluted flan ring on a baking sheet. (Invert baking sheet if it has a rim.)
2. Beat egg and sugar together in a small basin.
3. Place flour in a bowl; add fats, cut into small pieces and rub in with the fingertips until mixture resembles fine breadcrumbs. Add egg mixture and mix with a fork to form a firm dough. Turn out on to a floured board and knead until smooth.
4. Roll out pastry to a circle, 4cm (1½in) larger all around than flan ring. Support pastry on rolling pin and lift on to flan ring; gently ease pastry into flan ring and press into flutes. Roll off surplus pastry with rolling pin across top of flan ring; press pastry into flutes again with the fingers. Prick base with a fork.
5. To bake 'blind', line flan case with a circle of greaseproof paper and fill with baking beans or rice. Place in centre of oven. Bake for 15 minutes, to set pastry, then remove from oven; lift out paper and beans or rice. Return to oven and bake for a further 5 minutes. Leave to cool on a wire rack; place on a serving plate.

6. Scrub lemon; grate rind and squeeze juice. Place in a small saucepan, with cornflour, sugar and egg yolk; gradually stir in 125ml (¼ pint) water. Bring slowly to boil, stirring; cook for 1 minute. Immediately spread in base of cold flan case; leave to cool.
7. Chop chocolate. Place cornflour in a small saucepan; add a little of the measured milk and mix to a smooth paste. Add remaining milk, sugar and chocolate. Bring to boil slowly, stirring. Cook for 1 minute; pour over lemon filling in flan. Leave to cool.
8. Make up dessert topping mix, as directed on packet, using milk; place in a nylon piping bag fitted with a large star tube. Pipe 4 large whirls to mark off quarter sections of flan; between each large whirl, pipe 4 small stars of dessert topping. Spike the tops of the whirls and stars with the toasted, shredded almonds.

Fruit Bread

Mrs Nancy Gammie serves this to her guests with a hot drink in the evenings.

METRIC	IMPERIAL
150g plain flour	6oz plain flour
1 × 2.5ml spoon baking powder	½ level teaspoon baking powder
50g margarine	2oz margarine
100g castor sugar	4oz castor sugar
50g seedless raisins	2oz seedless raisins
50g currants	2oz currants
1 × 15ml spoon golden syrup or black treacle	1 level tablespoon golden syrup or black treacle
1 × 2.5ml spoon bicarbonate of soda	½ level teaspoon bicarbonate of soda
1 × 15ml spoon hot milk	1 tablespoon hot milk
1 egg	1 egg
6 × 15ml spoons cold milk	6 tablespoons cold milk

1. Prepare a cool oven (170 deg C, 325 deg F, Gas Mark 3). Line a ¾ litre (1½ pint) loaf tin with foil, or brush tin with melted fat and line with greaseproof paper; grease paper.
2. Place flour and baking powder in a bowl. Add margarine, cut into small pieces and rub in with the fingertips until mixture resembles fine breadcrumbs. Mix in sugar, raisins and currants. Make a well in centre and add syrup or treacle, levelling off spoon with a knife and making sure there is none on underside of spoon.
3. Dissolve bicarbonate of soda in the hot milk, stir well, then pour on to syrup mixture in bowl.
4. Beat egg and cold milk together; add to syrup mixture. Mix well, turn into tin; level top with back of spoon.
5. Bake in centre of oven for 1¼ to 1¾ hours. Test by pressing with the fingers. If cooked, loaf should spring back and have begun to shrink from sides of tin. Leave to cool in tin for 15 minutes, then turn out, remove foil or paper and leave bread to cool on a wire rack. Serve fruit bread thinly sliced and buttered if desired.

*Here are recipes for
every family celebration, from the
smartest dinner party to the most casual buffet. We found them
surprisingly economical to cook, yet every dish looks spectacular!*

Sweet and Sour Pork Chops

Mrs Susan Marr, from Gosforth, Newcastle upon Tyne, a finalist in one of our Cook of the Year competitions, provides us with this recipe.

For 4 portions

METRIC	IMPERIAL
2 medium-sized carrots	2 medium-sized carrots
2 medium-sized onions	2 medium-sized onions
2 medium-sized tomatoes	2 medium-sized tomatoes
1 medium-sized green pepper	1 medium-sized green pepper
100g button mushrooms	4oz button mushrooms
1 small (226g) can sliced pineapple	1 small (8¼oz) can sliced pineapple
50g sweet brown pickle	2oz sweet brown pickle
2 × 15ml spoons oil	2 tablespoons oil
4 loin pork chops	4 loin pork chops
1 × 15ml spoon cornflour	1 level tablespoon cornflour
1 chicken stock cube	1 chicken stock cube
3 × 15ml spoons malt vinegar	3 tablespoons malt vinegar
2 × 15ml spoons granulated sugar	2 level tablespoons granulated sugar
1 × 5ml spoon soy sauce	1 teaspoon soy sauce
Salt and pepper	Salt and pepper
200g long-grain rice	8oz long-grain rice
2 lemon twists	2 lemon twists

1. Peel and slice carrots and onions. Place tomatoes in a basin and cover with boiling water. Leave for 1 minute; drain, then peel and slice.
2. Cut green pepper in half lengthwise; discard seeds, core and white pith. Cut pepper into thin strips and place in a small saucepan. Cover with cold water and bring to boil; drain. Wash and slice mushrooms. Drain pineapple, reserving syrup; chop. Chop pickle.
3. Cook carrots in boiling, salted water for 10 to 15 minutes.
4. Heat oil in a frying pan; fry chops for 25 minutes, turning occasionally. Remove chops from pan and place in a warmed serving dish; keep warm.
5. Gently fry onions in fat remaining in pan for 5 minutes. Add the drained carrots, mushrooms and green pepper strips and cook for a further 5 minutes.

6. Stir in cornflour, 125ml (¼ pint) water, chicken stock cube, chopped pineapple and pineapple syrup, sliced tomatoes, vinegar, sugar, soy sauce, pickle and some salt and pepper. Bring to boil, stirring; cook gently for 10 minutes.
7. Meanwhile, cook rice in boiling, salted water for about 12 minutes. Test by pressing a grain between thumb and finger. Drain; rinse with boiling water. Arrange around chops.
8. Pour sauce over chops. Garnish with 2 lemon twists.

Noisettes of Lamb Garni

Mrs Ivy Smith, from Werrington in Peterborough cooked this recipe when she was a finalist in one of our Cook of the Year competitions.

For 4 portions

METRIC	IMPERIAL
¾kg joint best end neck of lamb	1½lb joint best end neck of lamb
1 medium-sized onion	1 medium-sized onion
1 medium-sized carrot	1 medium-sized carrot
1 beef stock cube	1 beef stock cube
MAITRE D'HOTEL BUTTER	MAITRE D'HOTEL BUTTER
50g butter	2oz butter
2 × 10ml spoons chopped parsley	2 rounded teaspoons chopped parsley
1 × 10ml spoon lemon juice	2 teaspoons lemon juice
¾kg potatoes	1½lb potatoes
Butter	Butter
Milk	Milk
Salt and pepper	Salt and pepper
4 large tomatoes	4 large tomatoes
200g mushrooms	8oz mushrooms
Oil	Oil
1 (226g) pack frozen peas	1 (½lb) pack frozen peas
1 × 15ml spoon plain flour	1 level tablespoon plain flour
Gravy browning (optional)	Gravy browning (optional)

1. Ask butcher to bone lamb. Peel and slice onion and carrot. Place onion, carrot and lamb bones in a saucepan; cover with water and bring to boil. Cover and simmer for 1 hour. Strain and measure 250ml (½ pint) stock; crumble and add stock cube. Cover and reserve.
2. Place lamb on a board, boned side uppermost; roll up and tie into 4 sections with string. Cut between string, to give 4 even-sized noisettes.
3. To make Maitre d'Hôtel Butter: cream butter, add parsley and lemon juice and mix well. Form into a roll, about 6cm (2½in) long, on a piece of wet greaseproof paper. Roll paper around butter and leave in refrigerator until required.
4. Peel potatoes and cook in boiling, salted water; drain, dry and mash. Beat in 25g (1oz) butter and sufficient milk to make a creamy texture. Taste and season with salt and pepper.
5. Prepare a moderate oven (190 deg C, 375 deg F, Gas Mark 5). Place potato in a large piping bag, fitted with a large star tube. Pipe potato around edge of a large, oblong, ovenproof dish.
6. Cut tomatoes in halves, scoop out pulp and reserve for gravy. Place 4 tomato shells down each long side of dish inside potato border. Bake in centre of oven for 10 to 15 minutes, or until tomatoes are soft and potato is lightly browned. Turn off oven.
7. Wash mushrooms; cut into quarters. Heat 1 × 10ml spoon (2 teaspoons) oil in a frying pan; fry mushrooms for 5 minutes. Remove from pan and place on dish, between tomato shells; replace dish in oven, to keep warm.
8. Fry noisettes for 6 to 8 minutes on each side; sprinkle with some salt and pepper. Place down centre of serving dish between lines of tomato shells; keep warm.
9. Cook peas as directed on pack, then drain.
10. Add flour to oil remaining in pan; gradually stir in stock and tomato pulp. Bring to boil, stirring; simmer for 3 minutes. Taste and season with salt and pepper; add a little gravy browning, if desired. Pour into a warmed gravy boat and keep warm.
11. To serve: place some peas in tomato shells; serve remainder separately. Cut Maitre d'Hôtel Butter into 4 slices; place 1 slice on each noisette. Serve immediately.

Flamenco Pork Chops

This recipe comes from Mrs Margaret Poppa, of Leeds, who was a finalist in one of our Cook of the Year competitions.

For 4 portions

METRIC	IMPERIAL
Half a small loaf of white bread	Half a small loaf of white bread
TOMATO SAUCE	TOMATO SAUCE
1 small onion	1 small onion
25g margarine	1oz margarine
1 large (396g) can tomatoes	1 large (14oz) can tomatoes
Boiling water	Boiling water
1 chicken stock cube	1 chicken stock cube
1 × 2.5ml spoon mixed dried herbs	½ level teaspoon mixed dried herbs
Salt and pepper	Salt and pepper
300g onions	¾lb onions
1 red pepper	1 red pepper
1 green pepper	1 green pepper
2 small courgettes	2 small courgettes
Margarine	Margarine
1 chicken stock cube	1 chicken stock cube
25g plain flour	1oz plain flour
1 egg	1 egg
4 loin pork chops	4 loin pork chops
6 sticks of celery	6 sticks of celery

1. Prepare a moderately hot oven (200 deg C, 400 deg F, Gas Mark 6).
2. Remove crust from bread; thinly slice bread and place on a baking sheet. Place in centre of oven and bake for 10 to 15 minutes, until bread is crisp and dry. Remove from oven; leave to cool.
3. To make tomato sauce: peel and finely chop onion. Melt 25g (1oz) margarine in a medium-sized saucepan. Add onion and fry gently for 5 minutes, until soft, but not browned.
4. Drain liquor from tomatoes and make up to 250ml (½ pint) with boiling water; add stock cube.
5. Chop tomatoes; add, with mixed dried herbs, to onion and cook for 1 minute. Stir in tomato stock; bring to boil, cover and simmer for 20 minutes. Taste and season with some salt and pepper. Cover sauce and reserve.
6. Peel and slice 300g (¾lb) onions. Cut peppers in halves lengthwise; discard seeds, core and white pith. Cut peppers into thin strips. Wash and dry courgettes; cut into thin slices.
7. Melt 50g (2oz) margarine in a frying pan; add onions and fry for 8 minutes, until cooked, but not browned. Remove onions from frying pan.
8. Melt 25g (1oz) margarine in frying pan; add sliced peppers and fry for 6 minutes, until tender. Remove peppers from frying pan.
9. Add sliced courgettes to frying pan and fry for 6 minutes, until tender. Replace onions and peppers; fry for a further 2 minutes. Place vegetables on a warmed serving plate; cover with foil and keep warm.
10. Meanwhile, grate bread to make breadcrumbs. Sieve breadcrumbs twice. Place 4 × 15ml spoons (4 tablespoons) breadcrumbs on a plate; add crumbled stock cube and mix together.
11. Place flour on a plate; beat egg on another plate.
12. Trim off excess fat from chops. Coat each chop in flour, then in beaten egg. Drain off excess egg and coat in breadcrumbs.
13. Melt 25g (1oz) margarine in frying pan; add chops. Cook for 20 to 25 minutes, turning once, until tender.
14. Wash and chop celery. Reheat sauce. Place chops on vegetables on serving plate; arrange chopped celery around. Pour a little of the tomato sauce over the chops; serve the remainder separately in a sauce boat.

GOLDEN
STUFFED
CHICKEN
*Recipe
on page 58*

Golden Stuffed Chicken

(pictured on pages 56/57)

Mrs Margaret Horne, from Isleworth in Middlesex, one of the finalists in a 1972 Cook of the Year competition, provides us with this recipe.

For 4 portions

METRIC	IMPERIAL
1 chicken (about 1½kg drawn weight)	1 chicken (about 3lb drawn weight)
1 medium-sized onion	1 medium-sized onion
Salt and pepper	Salt and pepper

STUFFING

METRIC	IMPERIAL
1 small onion	1 small onion
50g button mushrooms	2oz button mushrooms
Chicken liver from giblets	Chicken liver from giblets
25g butter	1oz butter
75g fresh white breadcrumbs	3oz fresh white breadcrumbs
1 × 2.5ml spoon grated lemon rind	½ level teaspoon grated lemon rind
1 × 10ml spoon lemon juice	2 teaspoons lemon juice
4 cocktail sticks	4 cocktail sticks
50g potato crisps	2oz potato crisps
1 clove of garlic	1 clove of garlic
50g butter	2oz butter

SAVOURY RICE

METRIC	IMPERIAL
150g long-grain rice	6oz long-grain rice
50g button mushrooms	2oz button mushrooms
1 chicken stock cube	1 chicken stock cube
400ml chicken stock	¾ pint chicken stock
50g frozen peas	2oz frozen peas

LEMON SAUCE

METRIC	IMPERIAL
1 small onion	1 small onion
25g butter	1oz butter
25g cornflour	½oz cornflour
1 chicken stock cube	1 chicken stock cube
250ml chicken stock	½ pint chicken stock
2 × 15ml spoons lemon juice	2 tablespoons lemon juice
1 × 5ml spoon grated lemon rind	1 level teaspoon grated lemon rind
1 × 5ml spoon soft brown sugar (light)	1 level teaspoon soft brown sugar (light)

GARNISH

METRIC	IMPERIAL
1 small lemon	1 small lemon
1 large tomato	1 large tomato
Parsley	Parsley
Paprika	Paprika

1. Remove giblets from chicken; reserve chicken liver for stuffing. Wash remaining giblets; place in a large saucepan.

2. Remove chicken skin; add to pan with the giblets.

3. Have front of chicken facing you. Using a small, sharp knife, cut flesh away from one side of breastbone; gradually cut away flesh from carcass, working towards the wing joint. Cut through wing joint, free flesh around joint; remove wing joint with breast.

4. Remove leg joint, by cutting against the carcass, through leg joint and down towards parson's nose, cutting the flesh free from the carcass. Repeat on other half of chicken.

5. Add carcass to saucepan. Peel and finely chop medium-sized onion; place in saucepan, with 1 litre (2 pints) water, 1 × 5ml spoon (1 level teaspoon) salt and a shake of pepper. Bring to boil, cover and simmer for 1 hour.

6. Cut off last two bones of wing joints. Slit flesh along remaining bone. Scrape back flesh, to expose bone; leave bone attached at bottom joint.

7. On one leg joint, slit flesh from drumstick up to joint; free bone by scraping back flesh. Cut through joint, to remove drumstick bone. Cut up the inside of the thigh bone and gradually cut away flesh, freeing bone at the thigh end and leaving attached at drumstick end. Repeat with other leg joint. Add removed bones to stock.

8. Dampen 2 sheets of greaseproof paper, place chicken joints between paper and flatten flesh with a rolling pin, taking care not to split flesh.

9. Prepare a moderate oven (180 deg C, 350 deg F, Gas Mark 4).

10. To make stuffing: peel and finely chop small onion. Wash mushrooms and chicken liver and chop finely.

11. Melt 25g (1oz) butter in a medium-sized saucepan; fry chopped ingredients for 5 minutes. Remove from heat; add breadcrumbs, lemon rind and juice, a little salt and a shake of pepper. Stir until mixture binds together.

12. Divide stuffing into 4 portions; place a portion on each chicken joint. Roll up joints firmly, leaving 1cm (½in) of bone protruding at one end of each, secure each joint with a cocktail stick.

13. Crush potato crisps; place crisps on plate.

14. Peel clove of garlic and place on a saucer, with a little salt. Using a round-ended knife, rub salt against garlic to crush clove.

15. Melt 50g (2oz) butter in a small saucepan; add garlic and salt. Brush each chicken joint with garlic butter; roll in crushed crisps. Arrange chicken in a shallow, ovenproof dish; strain remaining butter over chicken.

16. Place rice in a 1 litre (2 pint) casserole. Wash and slice mushrooms; add to casserole. Crumble in stock cube. Strain 400ml (¾ pint) chicken stock from saucepan over rice. Stir, then cover with a lid.

17. Place chicken and rice on shelf in centre of oven and cook for 35 to 45 minutes, until chicken is tender and rice has absorbed all the liquid.

18. Ten minutes before the end of cooking time, stir peas into rice.

19. To make lemon sauce: peel and finely chop small onion. Melt butter in a medium-sized saucepan; fry onion until tender, about 2 to 3 minutes. Stir in cornflour; remove from heat.

20. Crumble stock cube into a measuring jug; strain on

250ml (½ pint) stock from chicken bones and stir until stock cube has dissolved. Add to saucepan, with lemon juice and rind, sugar, a little salt and a shake of pepper. Return to heat, bring to boil, stirring continuously, and cook for 2 minutes. Taste and season with more salt and pepper, if necessary. Pour into a warmed sauce boat.

21. Cut 2 thin slices from lemon; cut each slice from edge to centre. Cut tomato into 12 wedges.

22. Arrange rice in a warmed serving dish; place chicken on top with bones pointing towards centre. Arrange lemon slices, in twists, on 2 opposite chicken bones and a sprig of parsley in centre. Arrange tomato wedges in between chicken joints and sprinkle chicken with paprika. Serve with lemon sauce.

Golden Chicken with Galantine

Mrs Mary Hamlin, from Abingdon, Oxfordshire, won first prize with this delicious dish in one of our Cook of the Year competitions.

For 4 portions

METRIC	IMPERIAL
2 medium-sized oranges	2 medium-sized oranges
1 chicken (about 1½kg drawn weight)	1 chicken (about 3lb drawn weight)
1 medium-sized carrot	1 medium-sized carrot
1 medium-sized turnip	1 medium-sized turnip
1 medium-sized onion	1 medium-sized onion
2 chicken stock cubes	2 chicken stock cubes
GALANTINE	GALANTINE
150g streaky bacon	6oz streaky bacon
Chicken liver from giblets	Chicken liver from giblets
50g button mushrooms	2oz button mushrooms
1 small onion	1 small onion
1 small cooking apple	1 small cooking apple
3 slices of white bread from a large loaf	3 slices white bread from a large loaf
1 sprig of parsley	1 sprig of parsley
½ × 2.5ml spoon mixed spice	¼ level teaspoon mixed spice
½ × 2.5ml spoon ground cinnamon	¼ level teaspoon ground cinnamon
1 egg	1 egg
Salt and pepper	Salt and pepper
Plain flour	Plain flour
1 × 5ml spoon paprika	1 level teaspoon paprika
2 × 15ml spoons oil	2 tablespoons oil
2 × 15ml spoons clear honey	2 level tablespoons clear honey
2 × 15ml spoons red wine vinegar	2 tablespoons red wine vinegar
200g long-grain rice	8oz long-grain rice
Juice of half a lemon	Juice of half a lemon
Watercress	Watercress

1. Scrub the oranges; grate the rind and squeeze juice from one orange. Place rind in a bowl; reserve for galantine and reserve the orange juice in another bowl.

2. Using a small, sharp knife or potato peeler, remove rind from second orange in long strips, taking care not to include any white pith; reserve. Using a sharp or serrated knife, cut pith from orange. Cut orange into 8 thin slices; reserve for garnish.

3. Cut chicken into 4 neat joints; leave in refrigerator. Place chicken trimmings in a large saucepan, with strips of orange rind. Reserve chicken liver for galantine; add remaining giblets to saucepan.

4. Peel and slice carrot, turnip and medium-sized onion; add to saucepan, with stock cubes and 1 litre (2 pints) cold water. Bring to boil, cover and simmer.

5. Meanwhile, make galantine: remove rind and bone from bacon; wash chicken liver and mushrooms. Peel small onion and apple. Cut apple into quarters; remove core. Remove crusts from bread; reserve for crumbs.

6. Finely mince bacon, liver, mushrooms, onion, apple, bread and parsley. Add to grated orange rind in bowl, with spices, egg, a little salt and a shake of pepper. Mix.

7. Turn out on to a piece of clean sheeting, lightly flour hands and shape into a sausage shape, about 15cm (6in) long. Roll up firmly in sheeting; tie ends firmly with string. Loosely sew up open edge with cotton.

8. Place galantine into stock in pan; cover and simmer for 45 minutes.

9. Prepare a moderately hot oven (200 deg C, 400 deg F, Gas Mark 6).

10. Mix together 2 × 15ml spoons (1 heaped tablespoon) flour, paprika, a little salt and shake of pepper on a plate. Coat chicken joints evenly with seasoned flour.

11. Heat oil in a large frying pan; fry chicken joints on both sides until evenly browned. Place in a roasting tin.

12. Add honey and vinegar to orange juice; mix well and pour over chicken. Cook just above centre of oven, until chicken is tender, about 35 minutes, basting occasionally with the liquor.

13. Place crusts of bread on a baking sheet; bake in oven until golden brown. Place crusts between 2 sheets of greaseproof paper; crush with a rolling pin, to make crumbs for coating galantine.

14. To cook rice: place rice in a large saucepan of boiling, salted water. Add lemon juice and cook for 12 minutes. Test by pressing a grain between thumb and finger. Drain and rinse with hot water. Place on a warmed serving dish; keep warm.

15. Remove galantine from stock; leave to cool for about 10 minutes. Remove chicken joints from oven, arrange on top of rice and keep warm.

16. Remove sheeting from galantine carefully; roll gantine in crumbs on greaseproof paper. Roll up tightly in paper; leave in a warm place for 10 minutes, to set. Cut into 8 slices.

17. Add 1 × 15ml spoon (1 level tablespoon) flour to roasting tin; blend with meat juices. Strain stock; add 250ml (½ pint) to roasting tin. Bring to boil, stirring, and cook for 2 minutes. Taste and season with salt and pepper; pour into a warmed sauce boat.

18. Garnish chicken with alternate slices of galantine and orange. Place a sprig of watercress on orange slices.

Grape Pavlova

Mrs Helen Lawrence, from Bangor, Northern Ireland, often serves this dessert when entertaining.

For 6 portions

METRIC	IMPERIAL
3 egg whites	3 egg whites
1 × 5ml spoon cornflour	1 level teaspoon cornflour
1 × 5ml spoon vinegar	1 teaspoon vinegar
1 × 5ml spoon vanilla essence	1 teaspoon vanilla essence
175g castor sugar	7oz castor sugar
250g grapes	½lb grapes
1 × 15ml spoon castor sugar (optional)	1 level tablespoon castor sugar (optional)
½ glass sherry (optional)	½ glass sherry (optional)
1 (142ml) carton double cream	1 (5 fluid oz) carton double cream

1. Prepare a cool oven (150 deg C, 300 deg F, Gas Mark 2). Wet a baking sheet and cover with greaseproof or silicone-treated paper.
2. Whisk egg whites until stiff but not dry.
3. Mix cornflour, vinegar and vanilla essence together and whisk into egg whites, with the sugar, a little at a time, until well blended. The mixture should be stiff, heavy and smooth.
4. Spread on the greaseproof paper to an even circle, about 2.5cm (1in) thick.
5. Place in oven and immediately turn heat down to very cool (140 deg C, 275 deg F, Gas Mark 1). Cook for 1 hour, when the pavlova should be crisp and marshmallow-like inside. Turn off oven and leave pavlova to cool without opening door. Remove from oven.
6. Cut grapes and remove pips. Place in a basin and sprinkle sugar and sherry over (if used). Cover and leave for 1 hour, stirring occasionally.
7. Strain grapes and place syrup, with cream, in a bowl; whisk until stiff. If sugar and sherry are omitted, add 2 × 15ml spoons (2 tablespoons) milk to cream before whisking. Carefully peel paper off base of pavlova. Place on a serving dish. Pile with cream and top with grapes.

Note: the pavlova will keep well for about a week in a closed tin. Decorate just before serving.

Vienna Steaks with French Onion Rings

(pictured opposite)

Mrs Gwen Penketh from Deganwy sent us this recipe.

For 4 portions

METRIC	IMPERIAL
VIENNA STEAKS	VIENNA STEAKS
1 large onion	1 large onion
½kg minced rump, shoulder or chuck steak	1lb minced rump, shoulder or chuck steak
1 × 10ml spoon chopped parsley	1 level dessertspoon chopped parsley
1 egg yolk	1 egg yolk
2 × 15ml spoons top of the milk	2 tablespoons top of the milk
1 × 5ml spoon salt	1 level teaspoon salt
Pepper	Pepper
BATTER	BATTER
100g plain flour	4oz plain flour
½ × 2.5ml spoon salt	¼ level teaspoon salt
1 egg white	1 egg white
125ml milk	¼ pint milk
Oil or fat for deep frying	Oil or fat for deep frying
PIQUANT GRAVY	PIQUANT GRAVY
Plain flour	Plain flour
250ml stock or vegetable water	½ pint stock or vegetable water
Worcestershire sauce	Worcestershire sauce
GARNISH	GARNISH
2 tomatoes	2 tomatoes
Parsley	Parsley

1. Peel and halve onion; cut one half into rings and finely chop remainder.
2. Place chopped onion, meat, parsley, egg yolk, top of the milk, salt and a little pepper in a bowl. Mix well, then turn out on to a floured board. Divide into 8 portions. Using a palette knife, shape into rounds.
3. To make batter: place flour and salt in a bowl. Make a well in centre of flour and add egg white. Gradually stir in milk and beat until smooth.
4. Melt a little fat or oil in a frying pan. Fry the steaks for 5 minutes on each side. Remove and keep hot. Drain excess fat from pan. Stir in 2 × 5ml spoons (1 heaped teaspoon) flour, then add stock, stirring continuously. Bring to boil and simmer for 3 minutes. Add a few drops Worcestershire sauce and season to taste. Keep warm.
5. Put deep fat pan on to heat. Dip onion rings in a little flour, then in batter. Fry in deep fat at 156 deg C (330 deg F) until golden brown and crisp; drain.
6. Arrange the steaks and onions rings on a warm serving dish; garnish with fried or grilled tomatoes and parsley. Serve with the piquant gravy and potato sticks.

VIENNA STEAKS WITH FRENCH ONION RINGS

Chicken Nairobi with Pulao Rice

Mr Robert Harvey, from Tunbridge Wells, Kent, won second prize in one of our Cook of the Year competitions with this delicious dish.

For 4 portions

METRIC	IMPERIAL
1 chicken (about 1½kg drawn weight)	1 chicken (about 3lb drawn weight)
12 whole cloves	12 whole cloves
Half a nutmeg	Half a nutmeg
1 × 5ml spoon mixed spice	1 level teaspoon mixed spice
Salt and pepper	Salt and pepper
Plain flour	Plain flour
1 medium-sized pineapple	1 medium-sized pineapple
1 lemon	1 lemon
1 chicken stock cube	1 chicken stock cube
25g butter	1oz butter
1 egg yolk	1 egg yolk
150ml single cream	¼ pint single cream

PULAO RICE	PULAO RICE
2 medium-sized onions	2 medium-sized onions
200g long-grain rice	8oz long-grain rice
1 × 2.5ml spoon turmeric	½ level teaspoon turmeric
1 chicken stock cube	1 chicken stock cube
100g mushrooms	¼lb mushrooms
50g sultanas	2oz sultanas
100g shelled almonds	4oz shelled almonds
1 × 15ml spoon oil	1 tablespoon oil
1 small (198g) can sweet corn kernels	1 small (7oz) can sweet corn kernels

GARNISH	GARNISH
1 lemon	1 lemon
1 medium-sized tomato	1 medium-sized tomato

1. Remove giblets, wash chicken and dry on kitchen paper. Remove skin from chicken. Divide chicken into 8 pieces: Remove both legs and split each at the joint, dividing them into thigh and drumstick. Remove wings, cutting a portion of breast with each wing. Split breast along bone; remove bone.

2. Place chicken skin, carcass and wing tips in a large frying pan. Fry gently, to extract the fat, for about 10 minutes. Remove from heat; remove skin, carcass and wing tips from pan.

3. Prepare spice mixture: crush cloves between 2 pieces of greaseproof paper with a rolling pin. Place in a large polythene bag. Grate nutmeg finely: add to bag. Add mixed spice, 1 × 2.5ml spoon (½ level teaspoon) salt, 1 × 2.5ml spoon (½ level teaspoon) pepper and 4 × 15ml spoons (2 rounded tablespoons) plain flour to bag; mix well.

4. Cut pineapple in half lengthwise, cutting straight through the leaves. With a sharp knife, cut out pineapple flesh, leaving shells scraped fairly clean. Reserve any juice that drains from pineapple. Cut pineapple flesh into small pieces. (Only half the flesh is required; reserve remainder in refrigerator for another meal.) Measure juice, which should be about 3 × 15ml spoons (3 tablespoons).

5. Scrub lemon. Cut in half and squeeze juice. Measure an equal quantity of lemon juice to pineapple juice; make up to 250ml (½ pint) with cold water.

6. Place one piece of chicken at a time in polythene bag; shake until coated with spice mixture. Place in chicken fat in frying pan; crumble over chicken stock cube. Cook over a gentle heat for 15 minutes, turning once.

7. Pour fruit juice over chicken pieces; bring to boil, cover and reduce heat. Simmer gently, stirring occasionally, for a further 20 minutes, until chicken pieces are just tender. Remove from heat; lift out chicken pieces and leave to cool on a plate. Remove bones from chicken; cut chicken into small pieces.

8. Strain off about 4 × 15ml spoons (4 tablespoons) fat from stock in frying pan; reserve for cooking rice. Pour remaining stock into a measuring jug; make up to 250ml (½ pint) with cold water. Make up spiced flour to 50g (1½oz) with more plain flour.

9. Melt butter in a saucepan; stir in spiced flour and cook for 2 minutes. Add stock, stirring continuously; bring to boil. Cook gently for 2 minutes. Taste and season with salt and pepper; remove from heat.

10. Place egg yolk in a small basin, with the cream; mix well. Whisk into sauce. Add chicken and pineapple pieces; mix well.

11. To make pulao rice: peel and finely chop onions. Place reserved chicken fat in a large frying pan. Add onions; fry gently for 5 minutes, without browning. Add rice, 1 × 10ml spoon (2 level teaspoons) salt, some pepper, turmeric and crumbled stock cube. Fry gently, stirring, for about 5 minutes, until rice is well coloured. Reduce heat, add ½ litre (1 pint) cold water, cover with a lid or foil; simmer for 15 minutes, stirring occasionally.

12. Wash, dry and quarter mushrooms; wash sultanas.

13. Place almonds in a small bowl; cover with boiling water and leave for 1 minute. Drain, remove skins and split in halves lengthwise.

14. Heat oil in a frying pan: add almonds. Fry gently, stirring, for about 5 minutes, until golden brown. Drain on kitchen paper. Drain liquor from sweet corn.

15. Add mushrooms, sultanas, sweet corn and half the almonds to rice. Stir well, cover and continue cooking for 5 minutes, until rice is tender and water absorbed. Test by pressing a grain between thumb and finger.

16. Place rice on a large, warmed serving dish, making 2 hollows, in which to place pineapple shells; keep hot.

17. To prepare garnish: hold lemon upright between finger and thumb. Using a small, sharp-pointed knife, make a zig-zag cut around middle of lemon into the centre. Gently pull lemon apart, cutting through centre, if necessary. Repeat with tomato.

18. Reheat chicken in sauce, but do not allow to boil. When hot, divide mixture between pineapple shells. Place, side by side, on rice; sprinkle remaining almonds over. Arrange lemon and tomato halves on serving dish.

Pâté Stuffed Chicken

Mrs Peggy Morgan, from Carmarthen, won first prize in one of our Cook of the Year competitions.

For 4 portions

METRIC	IMPERIAL
1 chicken (about 1½kg drawn weight)	1 chicken (about 3lb drawn weight)
3 hard-boiled eggs	3 hard-boiled eggs
50g streaky bacon	2oz streaky bacon
1 small onion	1 small onion
Oil	Oil
Butter	Butter
50g fresh white breadcrumbs	2oz fresh white breadcrumbs
1 × 15ml spoon chopped parsley	1 level tablespoon chopped parsley
Pinch of dried thyme	Pinch of dried thyme
200g liver sausage	½lb liver sausage
Grated rind of half a lemon	Grated rind of half a lemon
1 × 10ml spoon lemon juice	2 teaspoons lemon juice
Salt and pepper	Salt and pepper
1 × 10ml spoon plain flour	2 level teaspoons plain flour
SAUCE	SAUCE
50g mushrooms	2oz mushrooms
25g butter	½oz butter
150ml white wine	¼ pint white wine
1 × 15ml spoon cornflour	1 level tablespoon cornflour
1 chicken stock cube	1 chicken stock cube
2 × 15ml spoons single cream	2 tablespoons single cream
Salt and pepper	Salt and pepper
GARNISH	GARNISH
1 lemon	1 lemon
Parsley	Parsley
100g frozen peas	¼lb frozen peas
2 tomatoes	2 tomatoes
4 slices white bread from a small loaf	4 slices white bread from a small loaf
Oil	Oil

1. Reserve chicken liver; place remainder of giblets in a medium-sized saucepan. Rinse and dry chicken.

2. To bone chicken: place chicken, breast downwards, with neck end facing away from you, on a board. Using a large, sharp knife, cut skin along backbone, from neck to tail. Cut off wing tips and tail; cut through bottom leg joint. Using a small, sharp knife, starting at neck end, gradually work flesh away from bones. When joint, where wing joins body of chicken, is exposed, cut through joint. Scrape down wing bones, turning wings inside out. When bones are removed from wings, continue working down body, making sure skin is not pierced. When leg joint is exposed, cut through joint and work down legs, turning them inside out, as for wings. When the meat is attached to carcass only by the breastbone, gently ease the meat away from the bone with a knife.

3. Add chicken bones to giblets in saucepan; cover with water. Bring to boil, cover; simmer 1½ to 2 hours.

4. Prepare a moderately hot oven (200 deg C, 400 deg F, Gas Mark 6). Shell and slice eggs.

5. Remove rind and bone from bacon; chop bacon. Peel and chop onion. Slice chicken liver.

6. Heat 1 × 15ml spoon (1 tablespoon) oil and a knob of butter in a frying pan. Fry chicken liver for 3 minutes; remove from pan and reserve. Fry onion and bacon until tender, but not browned, about 5 minutes. Add breadcrumbs, parsley and thyme; mix well.

7. Place liver sausage in a bowl; mash with a fork. Add breadcrumb mixture, lemon rind and juice, 1 × 2.5ml spoon (½ level teaspoon) salt, shake of pepper; mix.

8. Lay chicken flat on a board, skin side downwards, leaving legs and wings turned inside out. Spread half the liver sausage mixture down centre of chicken, over breast meat; arranged sliced eggs on top and sliced liver over eggs. Top with remaining liver sausage mixture; fold chicken over, to enclose stuffing. Using thin string and a trussing needle (or poultry pins), close skin of chicken, leaving about 15cm (6in) string each end.

9. Place chicken, join downwards, in a roasting tin. Mix flour and some salt and pepper together; sprinkle over chicken. Melt a knob of butter and 1 × 15ml spoon (1 tablespoon) oil together; pour over chicken. Cook chicken in centre of oven for 1 hour or until golden.

10. To make sauce: wash and trim the mushrooms. Slice 4 mushrooms; reserve centre slices for garnish. Chop end pieces and remaining mushrooms and stalks finely. Melt butter in a small saucepan; fry mushroom slices for 2 to 3 minutes. Remove from saucepan; drain on kitchen paper. Add chopped mushrooms to fat in pan; fry, stirring occasionally, for 3 minutes.

11. Add white wine, bring to boil and cook quickly until wine has reduced by half, about 4 minutes.

12. Mix cornflour and 1 × 15ml spoon (1 tablespoon) water together. Gradually blend in 250ml (½ pint) chicken stock (from bones). Stir into mushroom and wine mixture; add stock cube. Bring to boil, stirring; cook for 3 minutes. Just before serving, stir in cream; taste and season. Reheat, but do not boil.

13. To make lemon basket: make 2 parallel cuts, slightly apart, half way through lemon along length, one on either side of and at right angles to first cuts, leaving centre strip attached. Remove wedges formed. Using a sharp, pointed knife, cut out lemon flesh, to form a basket and handle. Fill basket with sprigs of parsley.

14. To make tomato cups: cook peas, as directed on pack. Cut tomatoes in halves. Using a teaspoon, scoop out centres. Fill cups with peas and keep warm.

15. Using a heart-shaped cutter, cut out a croûte from each slice of bread. Heat a little oil in a frying pan; fry croûtes until golden; drain. Sprinkle with parsley.

16. To serve: place chicken on a large, warmed serving dish. Pull out string from one end (or remove poultry pins). Arrange sliced mushrooms along centre of chicken; croûtes and tomato cups at each side and lemon basket at one end. Pour sauce into a warmed gravy boat.

63

SEVILLE-GLAZED
CHICKEN WITH
LEMON RICE
*Recipe on
page 67*

Poulet d'Or

(pictured on back cover)

Mrs Gloria Heane, from Market Harborough, in Leicestershire, sent us this spectacular dish.

For 4 to 6 portions

METRIC	IMPERIAL
1 chicken (about 1½kg drawn weight)	1 chicken (about 3lb drawn weight)

STOCK

METRIC	IMPERIAL
Giblets from chicken	Giblets from chicken
1 small carrot	1 small carrot
1 small onion	1 small onion
1 stick of celery	1 stick of celery
1 chicken stock cube	1 chicken stock cube
1 × 2.5ml spoon mixed dried herbs	½ level teaspoon mixed dried herbs
1 bay leaf	1 bay leaf
Salt and pepper	Salt and pepper

HERB AND ONION STUFFING

METRIC	IMPERIAL
50g fresh white breadcrumbs	2oz fresh white breadcrumbs
1 × 5ml spoon mixed dried herbs	1 level teaspoon mixed dried herbs
1 × 5ml spoon chopped parsley	1 level teaspoon chopped parsley
½ × 2.5ml spoon dried sage	¼ level teaspoon dried sage
25g suet	1oz suet
1 × 2.5ml spoon grated lemon rind	½ level teaspoon grated lemon rind
4 × 15ml spoons minced onion	2 heaped tablespoons minced onion
1 egg	1 egg

SAVOURY CRUST

METRIC	IMPERIAL
450g plain flour	1lb plain flour
1 × 2.5ml spoon mixed dried herbs	½ level teaspoon mixed dried herbs
1 × 5ml spoon minced onion	½ rounded teaspoon minced onion
100g lard	4oz lard
25g margarine	1oz margarine
1 chicken stock cube	1 chicken stock cube
2 cloves	2 cloves

GOLDEN EGGS

METRIC	IMPERIAL
4 large pork sausages	4 large pork sausages
1 × 10ml spoon minced onion	1 rounded teaspoon minced onion
100g button mushrooms	4oz button mushrooms
1 × 10ml spoon plain flour	2 level teaspoons plain flour
2 eggs	2 eggs
Oil for frying	Oil for frying

CHICKEN LIVER SAUCE

1 rasher streaky bacon	1 rasher streaky bacon
2 button mushrooms	2 button mushrooms
25g sliced onion	1oz sliced onion
1 chicken liver	1 chicken liver
25g butter	1oz butter
2 × 15ml spoons cornflour	2 level tablespoons cornflour
1 × 2.5ml spoon mixed dried herbs	½ level teaspoon mixed dried herbs
Grated rind of quarter of a lemon	Grated rind of quarter of a lemon
1 × 5ml spoon lemon juice	1 teaspoon lemon juice
1 × 5ml spoon granulated sugar	1 level teaspoon granulated sugar
150ml single cream	5 fluid oz single cream
Chopped parsley	Chopped parsley
Paprika	Paprika
Celery tops	Celery tops
3 or 4 chicken tail feathers	3 or 4 chicken tail feathers

1. Remove giblets from chicken; wash and place in a medium-sized saucepan.

2. Peel carrot and onion; chop finely and add to saucepan.

3. Wash and chop celery; add to saucepan, with stock cube, herbs, bay leaf, a little salt, a shake of pepper and ½ litre (1 pint) cold water. Bring to boil, cover and simmer for 2 hours. Strain, reserve the stock and the chicken liver for the sauce.

4. To make stuffing: mix all ingredients, except egg, in a basin. Add a little salt and a shake of pepper. Beat egg and add a little to bind stuffing, keeping mixture fairly dry. Reserve remaining egg for glazing.

5. Wipe chicken inside and out with kitchen paper. Press stuffing into neck end of chicken; place any remaining stuffing in body cavity. Tie parson's nose and legs together firmly with string.

6. Brush chicken all over with a little beaten egg and sprinkle with salt and pepper. Place the chicken on a baking sheet.

7. Bend a medium-sized, thin metal skewer into a broad 'U' shape. Secure one end of skewer into the neck end of chicken, just below breast bone, and the other end into base of chicken, so that rounded part of skewer protrudes by about 5cm (2in) in front.

8. Prepare a fairly hot oven (220 deg C, 425 deg F, Gas Mark 7).

9. To make savoury crust: place flour, 1 × 5ml spoon (1 level teaspoon) salt, a shake of pepper, herbs and onion in a bowl. Place fats, stock cube and 225ml (8 fluid oz) of water in a saucepan. Heat until fats have melted. Make a well in centre of flour, add liquid and beat with a wooden spoon, to form a firm dough. Leave to cool slightly; turn out on to a lightly floured board and knead with the fingers. Cut pastry in half.

10. Cut 1 half of pastry in 2; form 1 piece into a ball and press over top of skewer in chicken, to represent head; cut the other piece of pastry into 3 equal portions. Roll

66

out 1 portion, so that it is large enough to cover ends of chicken legs, to represent tail. Roll out remaining 2 portions of pastry; cut out 2 wing shapes. Roll out reserved half of pastry, so that it is large enough to cover chicken. Cut out 2 holes for head and tail to go through. Support the pastry over rolling pin and cover the chicken, tucking the pastry jacket well under all around the chicken.

11. Mould pastry over the skewer into neck, beak and comb shapes with the fingers. Place cloves in position for eyes. Brush pastry all over with some beaten egg; press wings in position on each side of chicken, using the point of a teaspoon and a small knife to attach them securely.

12. Bake chicken in centre of oven for 5 minutes, then cover head and tail with foil; cook for a further 15 minutes. Reduce oven temperature to moderate (180 deg C, 350 deg F, Gas Mark 4). Cover chicken with greaseproof paper and cook for a further 1¼ to 1½ hours.

13. To make golden eggs: remove skins from sausages. Place sausagemeat in a basin, with minced onion. Wash mushrooms, mince finely and add to basin, with a little salt and a shake of pepper. Divide mixture into 4 portions; dip each portion into flour and mould them into egg shapes.

14. Hard boil eggs for 10 minutes; crack and leave to cool in cold water. Shell and dry on kitchen paper.

15. Cut eggs in halves lengthwise. Place yolks in a sieve over a basin; rub through sieve with a wooden spoon. Cut egg whites in halves twice more, to represent petals for garnish.

16. Heat oil in a frying pan; fry sausage eggs for 4 to 5 minutes on each side, until golden brown and sausage has cooked through. Drain on kitchen paper; brush tops with a little of the remaining beaten egg and then sprinkle with some of the sieved egg yolk. Keep the sausage eggs warm.

17. To make chicken liver sauce: remove rind and bone from bacon; wash mushrooms. Mince bacon, mushrooms and onion together finely, with reserved chicken liver.

18. Melt butter in a saucepan; fry minced ingredients for 2 to 3 minutes. Add cornflour; stir in 375ml (¾ pint) reserved chicken stock. Bring to boil, stirring, and cook for 2 minutes. Add herbs, lemon rind and juice and sugar. Cover and simmer the sauce for about 15 to 20 minutes.

19. Reserve 1 × 15ml spoon (1 tablespoon) cream; just before serving, add remaining cream to the sauce. Heat gently, but do not boil. Strain into a warmed sauce boat. Swirl in reserved cream, then sprinkle with chopped parsley.

20. Place chicken on a warmed serving dish. Arrange 8 egg white petals, in a circle, at each corner of front of dish, to form flowers. Pile 1 × 5ml (1 teaspoonful) of sieved yolk in centre of each; sprinkle with paprika.

21. Place eggs around front of chicken. Arrange celery tops on dish along each side of chicken and place the tail feathers in position.

Seville-glazed Chicken (pictured on pages 64/65)

Mrs Elaine Brocklehurst, from St Helens, Merseyside, sent us her prize-winning recipe.

For 4 portions

METRIC	IMPERIAL
4 chicken joints	4 chicken joints
Salt	Salt
25g butter	½oz butter
1 small onion	1 small onion
4 medium-sized mushrooms (cups)	4 medium-sized mushrooms (cups)
1 × 10ml spoon curry powder	2 level teaspoons curry powder
3 × 15ml spoons plain flour	3 level tablespoons plain flour
1 chicken stock cube	1 chicken stock cube
375ml boiling water	¾ pint boiling water
2 × 15ml spoons chunky marmalade	2 level tablespoons chunky marmalade
LEMON RICE	**LEMON RICE**
1 medium-sized lemon	1 medium-sized lemon
200g long-grain rice	8oz long-grain rice
1 chicken stock cube	1 chicken stock cube
1 × 5ml spoon salt	1 level teaspoon salt
GARNISH	**GARNISH**
2 × 15ml spoons frozen peas	1 heaped tablespoon frozen peas
4 slices of orange	4 slices of orange

1. Prepare oven (200 deg C, 400 deg F, Gas Mark 6).

2. Cut each piece of chicken in half through the joint, cutting some of breast with each wing; sprinkle with salt.

3. Melt butter in a frying pan; fry chicken pieces, until browned. Place them in a 1½ litre (3 pint) casserole. Cover; cook in centre oven for 30 minutes.

4. Peel and chop onion. Wash mushrooms, remove stalks and chop; reserve mushroom cups for garnish. Add onion to fat in pan and cook for 2 minutes. Stir in mushroom stalks; cook for 1 minute. Stir in curry powder and flour; cook for 1 minute. Stir in stock cube dissolved in boiling water. Bring to boil, stirring; add marmalade and stir well.

5. Pour sauce over chicken; return to oven and cook, uncovered, for a further 30 minutes, until tender.

6. To make lemon rice: scrub lemon; grate rind finely and squeeze juice. Place in a frying pan with rice, crumbled stock cube, salt and ¾ litre (1⅓ pints) water. Bring to boil; cover and simmer for 15 minutes, until liquid has been absorbed and rice is tender. Cook peas and mushroom cups in boiling water for 5 minutes; drain.

7. To serve: place rice around edge of a warmed serving dish. Arrange chicken in centre and pour sauce over. Fill mushroom cups with peas. Cut into centre of each orange slice and twist. Arrange these as garnish.

MALLOW MEDLEYS

Mallow Medleys

(pictured left)

Mrs Pat Williams, from Evesham in Worcestershire, made this dessert at the finals of one of our Cook of the Year competitions.

For 6 portions

METRIC	IMPERIAL
300g shortbread biscuits	12oz shortbread biscuits
150g marshmallows	6oz marshmallows
150g margarine	6oz margarine
3 × 15ml spoons milk	3 tablespoons milk
50g soft brown sugar (dark)	1½oz soft brown sugar (dark)
6 × 15ml spoons sweet sherry	6 tablespoons sweet sherry
100g cooking chocolate	4oz cooking chocolate
3 eggs	3 eggs
1 large (284g) can cream	1 large (10oz) can cream

1. Crush biscuits between 2 sheets of greaseproof paper, using a rolling pin.

2. Cut marshmallows and margarine into small pieces. Place in a medium-sized saucepan, with milk and sugar. Heat gently, stirring continuously, until marshmallows have melted. Bring to boil, remove from heat and stir in half the biscuit crumbs; mix well. Leave to cool slightly; divide mixture equally between 6 individual serving glasses. Level tops with back of a teaspoon and leave until set.

3. Place remaining biscuit crumbs in a basin; add sherry. Mix well, to form a paste, and divide equally between glasses. Spread mixture evenly over first layer.

4. Break 75g (3oz) chocolate into small pieces and place in a basin. Bring a small saucepan of water to the boil; remove from heat and place basin on top. Leave for 5 to 6 minutes, stirring occasionally, until chocolate has melted.

5. Separate eggs. Place whites in a clean, grease-free basin and beat yolks into melted chocolate; remove basin from saucepan.

6. Whisk egg whites until stiff, but not dry. Using a metal spoon, lightly fold into chocolate mixture until well mixed. Spoon chocolate mousse equally between glasses and chill thoroughly, until set.

7. Pour contents of can of cream into a basin. Stir until smooth and spread evenly over top of chocolate mousse in each glass.

8. Break remaining chocolate into small pieces and place in a basin; place over saucepan of hot water. Leave for 2 to 3 minutes, until chocolate has melted. Spoon melted chocolate into a small greaseproof paper piping bag. Fold down top and snip a small piece from point. Pipe a treble clef musical motif on top of cream on each glass, to decorate.

Note: this dessert can also be made in one large glass bowl, if preferred, for a dramatic effect.

Apple and Apricot Amber

(pictured below)

Mrs Christina Mann, from Whitley Bay, Northumberland, sent us this tempting recipe.

For 4 to 6 portions

METRIC	IMPERIAL
1kg cooking apples	2lb cooking apples
200g granulated sugar	8oz granulated sugar
25g butter	1oz butter
4 × 15ml spoons apricot jam	4 level tablespoons apricot jam
Demerara sugar	Demerara sugar
125ml double cream	4 fluid oz double cream
1 × 15ml spoon top of the milk	1 tablespoon top of the milk

DECORATION	DECORATION
Apricot jam	Apricot jam
3 glacé cherries	3 glacé cherries

1. Peel, core and slice apples. Place in a saucepan with 8 × 15ml spoons (8 tablespoons) water and granulated sugar. Cook over a low heat, stirring continuously, until soft and thick.

2. Remove from heat and add butter and jam. Mix well and pour into a 1 litre (2 pint) ovenproof dish; leave the mixture to cool.

3. Prepare a moderate grill; remove grill pan. Sprinkle sufficient demerara sugar on top to cover apple mixture thickly; grill until sugar has caramelised. Remove from grill and leave until cold.

4. Place cream and milk in a basin and whisk until just thick. Pile 12 × 10ml spoons (12 dessertspoons) of cream around edge of dish; decorate cream with apricot jam and halved glacé cherries. Serve cold.

APPLE AND APRICOT AMBER

Noisettes of Lamb Hunters Style

Miss Janet Bell, from Penn in Wolverhampton, provides us with this recipe. She was a finalist in one of our Cook of the Year competitions.

For 4 portions

METRIC	IMPERIAL
HUNTERS' SAUCE	**HUNTERS' SAUCE**
25g streaky bacon	1oz streaky bacon
50g celery	2oz celery
2 medium-sized onions	2 medium-sized onions
1 large (396g) can tomatoes	1 large (14oz) can tomatoes
1 clove of garlic	1 clove of garlic
Salt	Salt
2 parsley stalks	2 parsley stalks
25g margarine	½oz margarine
25g plain flour	½oz plain flour
1 beef stock cube	1 beef stock cube
1 × 2.5ml spoon mixed dried herbs	½ level teaspoon mixed dried herbs
A knob of butter	A knob of butter
Pepper	Pepper
NOISETTES	NOISETTES
Parsley	Parsley
100g mushrooms	4oz mushrooms
1 clove of garlic	1 clove of garlic
Salt	Salt
1 × 2.5ml spoon mixed dried herbs	½ level teaspoon mixed dried herbs
1 egg	1 egg
A little seasoned flour	A little seasoned flour
¾kg boned best end neck of lamb	1½lb boned best end neck of lamb
8 wooden cocktail sticks	8 wooden cocktail sticks
Pepper	Pepper
GARNISH	GARNISH
1 medium-sized aubergine	1 medium-sized aubergine
1 medium-sized onion	1 medium-sized onion
4 large tomatoes	4 large tomatoes
1 × 15ml spoon oil	1 tablespoon oil
25g butter	1oz butter
1 × 2.5ml spoon mixed dried herbs	½ level teaspoon mixed dried herbs
Salt and pepper	Salt and pepper
SAVOURY RICE	SAVOURY RICE
2 medium-sized onions	2 medium-sized onions
1 clove of garlic	1 clove of garlic
Salt	Salt
1 chicken stock cube	1 chicken stock cube
250ml boiling water	½ pint boiling water
1 small (198g) can red peppers	1 small (7oz) can red peppers
50g butter	2oz butter
100g long-grain rice	4oz long-grain rice
Pepper	Pepper
2 × 15ml spoons oil	2 tablespoons oil
25g butter	1oz butter
Sprigs of parsley	Sprigs of parsley

1. To make sauce: remove rind and bone from bacon; cut bacon into small pieces. Wash, trim and thinly slice celery. Peel and chop onions. Drain liquor from can of tomatoes into a measuring jug; make up to 400ml (¾ pint) with water. Peel clove of garlic and place on a saucer with 1 × 2.5ml spoon (½ level teaspoon) salt. Using a round-ended knife, rub salt against garlic to crush clove. Chop parsley stalks.

2. Melt margarine in a saucepan; gently fry bacon, celery and onion for 10 minutes. Stir in flour. Add tomato liquor; bring to boil, stirring. Crumble and add stock cube, garlic, chopped parsley stalks, drained tomatoes and mixed dried herbs. Cover and simmer for 1 hour.

3. Sieve sauce into a bowl; add knob of butter. Taste and season with salt and pepper, if necessary. Return to saucepan; cover and reserve.

4. To prepare noisettes: chop enough parsley to yield 2 × 15ml spoons (1 rounded tablespoon). Wash and finely chop mushrooms. Peel clove of garlic and crush with 1 × 2.5ml spoon (½ level teaspoon) salt, as in step 1. Mix parsley, mushrooms, garlic and mixed dried herbs together; place on a sheet of greaseproof paper. Beat egg and place in a shallow dish. Place the seasoned flour on a plate.

5. Place boned joint of lamb on a board, boned side uppermost. Cut into 8 equal slices, on the slant; trim off corner ends and discard. Using a rolling pin, batten out each slice slightly, form each into a round and secure with a wooden cocktail stick. Sprinkle with salt and pepper.

6. Thoroughly coat noisettes in seasoned flour, then in beaten egg. Press each side into mushroom mixture, to coat; put to one side.

7. To prepare garnish: wash and cut aubergine into small dice. Peel and chop onion. Place tomatoes in a basin and cover with boiling water. Leave for 1 minute; drain, then peel. Cut in halves; remove pulp and discard.

8. Heat oil and butter in a small saucepan and gently fry aubergine, onion, mixed dried herbs, 1 × 2.5ml spoon (½ level teaspoon) salt and a shake of pepper for 10 minutes. Taste and season with more salt and pepper, if necessary; keep mixture hot.

9. To make savoury rice: prepare a hot oven (220 deg C, 425 deg F, Gas Mark 7). Peel and chop onions. Peel clove of garlic and crush with 1 × 2.5ml spoon (½ level teaspoon) salt, as in step 1. Add chicken stock cube to boiling water. Drain red peppers; cut into small dice. Melt 25g (1oz) butter in a medium-sized saucepan; gently fry onion and garlic for 2 to 3 minutes. Add rice and stock, 1 × 5ml spoon (1 level teaspoon) salt and a shake of pepper. Transfer mixture to a casserole; cover and cook in centre of oven for 17 minutes, or until rice is

tender. Test by pressing a grain between thumb and finger.

10. Gently stir in remaining 25g (1oz) butter and diced red peppers. Spoon rice on to a warmed serving dish. Arrange tomato halves around edge of dish and fill with aubergine and onion mixture; keep warm in oven.

11. Reheat sauce. Heat 2 × 15ml spoons (2 tablespoons) oil and 25g (1oz) butter in a frying pan; gently fry noisettes for 5 minutes on each side. Drain; place noisettes on rice, overlapping, in centre of dish. Pour a little sauce over the noisettes and garnish with parsley. Place remaining sauce in a warmed sauce boat and serve separately.

Cherry Meringue Crunch

Mrs Daphne Trott, from Weymouth in Dorset, was a finalist in one of our Cook of the Year competitions with this dish.

For 4 to 6 portions

METRIC	IMPERIAL
150g digestive biscuits	6oz digestive biscuits
100g butter	4oz butter
25g castor sugar	1oz castor sugar
1 (397g) can cherry pie filling	1 (14½oz) can cherry pie filling

MERINGUE	MERINGUE
1 egg white	1 egg white
50g castor sugar	2oz castor sugar

1. Prepare a moderate oven (180 deg C, 350 deg F, Gas Mark 4). Brush a 19cm (7½in) sponge flan tin with oil or melted fat.

2. Crush digestive biscuits with a rolling pin between 2 sheets of greaseproof paper. Place butter in a small saucepan; heat until melted. Remove from heat; stir in biscuit crumbs and 25g (1oz) castor sugar. Mix well; press evenly into flan tin. Bake in centre of oven for 10 to 15 minutes. Leave to cool before removing from tin. Reduce oven heat to cool (170 deg C, 325 deg F, Gas Mark 3).

3. Place flan on an ovenproof serving dish. Pile cherry pie filling in centre.

4. Place egg white in a clean, grease-free bowl. Whisk until stiff, but not dry. Whisk in half the sugar; fold in remainder, cutting through mixture with a metal spoon, until all the sugar has been incorporated.

5. Place meringue in a piping bag, fitted with a large star tube. Pipe 7 whirls around edge of flan. Bake in centre of oven for a further 15 to 20 minutes, or until the meringue is golden brown. Serve either hot or cold.

Malakoff

Mrs E Brocklehurst, from St Helens, Merseyside, won second prize in one of our Cook of the Year competitions with this dessert.

For 4 portions

METRIC	IMPERIAL
50g blanched almonds	1½oz blanched almonds
50g margarine	2oz margarine
50g icing sugar	1½oz icing sugar
1 egg	1 egg
50g cottage cheese	2oz cottage cheese
1 × 10ml spoon rum	1 dessertspoon rum
150ml natural yoghourt	5 fluid oz natural yoghourt
2 × 15ml spoons milk	2 tablespoons milk
22 sponge finger biscuits (1½ packets)	22 sponge finger biscuits (1½ packets)

1. Line base of a 15cm (6in) round, loose-based cake tin with foil; line side with a 4cm (1½in) strip of foil.

2. Prepare a moderate grill. Place almonds in grill pan; toast until golden brown. Reserve 6 almonds for decoration and chop remainder.

3. Cream margarine and icing sugar together in a bowl until light and fluffy. Separate egg; place white in a clean, grease-free basin and beat egg yolk into margarine and sugar mixture.

4. Sieve cottage cheese; beat into the mixture in bowl, with the rum.

5. Stir yoghourt. Fold in half the yoghourt; reserve remainder for decoration. Whisk egg white until stiff, but not dry; fold egg white and chopped almonds into mixture in bowl.

6. Place milk in a saucer; dip 5 sponge finger biscuits in milk and place on base of prepared tin. Spread half the almond mixture over biscuits. Dip 5 more sponge finger biscuits in milk and place on top of mixture in tin (in opposite direction to first 5). Spread remaining almond mixture on top. Leave in refrigerator to set.

7. Invert tin on to a serving plate; carefully remove tin and foil.

8. Cut remaining sponge finger biscuits in halves. Press flat side of each around side. Spread reserved yoghourt over the top and decorate with reserved almonds.

Caribbean Cake

(pictured below)

Mrs E Lazenby, from Bagshot in Berkshire, was a finalist in one of our Cook of the Year competitions, where she made this cake.

METRIC
CAKE
100g soft margarine
100g castor sugar
2 eggs
2 × 15ml spoons milk
2 × 15ml spoons boiling water
125g self-raising flour
1 × 5ml spoon baking powder

FILLING
4 × 15ml spoons rum
50g sultanas
100g plain chocolate
25g margarine
1 × 5ml spoon instant coffee
1 × 15ml spoon castor sugar
4 × 15ml spoons boiling water
4 × 15ml spoons apricot jam

300ml double cream

IMPERIAL
CAKE
4oz soft margarine
4oz castor sugar
2 eggs
2 tablespoons milk
2 tablespoons boiling water
5oz self-raising flour
1 level teaspoon baking powder

FILLING
4 tablespoons rum
2oz sultanas
4oz plain chocolate
½oz margarine
1 level teaspoon instant coffee
1 level tablespoon castor sugar
4 tablespoons boiling water
2 rounded tablespoons apricot jam

10 fluid oz double cream

1. Prepare a moderate oven (180 deg C, 350 deg F, Gas Mark 4). Brush 2, 18cm (7in) sandwich tins with melted fat or oil. Line bases with greaseproof paper, then grease the paper.

2. Place margarine and 100g (4oz) castor sugar in a bowl. Beat together with a wooden spoon until light and fluffy. Beat eggs together; add gradually, beating well after each addition. Mix together milk and water; add to mixture, with flour and baking powder. Fold into mixture carefully, using a metal spoon, to make a soft dropping consistency.

3. Divide mixture evenly between tins; level tops with back of a metal spoon.

4. Bake in centre of oven for 20 to 30 minutes. Test cakes by pressing with the fingers. If cooked, cakes should spring back and have begun to shrink from sides of tins. Leave cakes to cool in tins for 5 minutes; loosen edges with a round-ended knife, turn out and leave to cool completely on a wire rack.

5. Place rum and sultanas in a basin; leave to soak.

6. To make chocolate curls: place chocolate, patterned side downwards, on a working surface. Holding a long, sharp knife between the hands, at the point and handle, shave off thin layers of chocolate, at an angle, to form about 20 curls. Keep in refrigerator.

7. Place remaining chocolate and 25g (½oz) margarine in a dry basin over a saucepan of hot, but not boiling, water. Stir occasionally, until chocolate has melted. Remove basin from heat.

8. In another basin, blend together coffee, 1 × 15ml spoon (1 tablespoon) castor sugar and 4 × 15ml spoons (4 tablespoons) boiling water; leave to cool.

9. Using a sharp knife, cut 1 cake in half horizontally. Spread inside of both halves thinly with apricot jam.

10. Crumble remaining cake finely; mix one third of crumbs with rum and sultanas. Stir another third of crumbs into melted chocolate and remaining third into coffee syrup.

11. Spread rum and sultana mixture over bottom layer of cake, making sure mixture is level. Cover with a chocolate layer; top with a coffee layer. Replace top of cake and press firmly.

12. Place cream in a bowl; whisk until cream just holds its shape. Place 100ml (4 rounded tablespoons) cream in a piping bag fitted with a medium-sized star tube.

13. Spread remaining cream over top and side of cake, to coat evenly. Smooth with a palette knife. Place cake on a serving plate.

14. Pipe stars of cream around base of cake and around

CARIBBEAN
CAKE

edge. Arrange chocolate curls on top of cake making an artistic decoration.

Note: this cake improves with keeping. Make and fill the cake, leave overnight, then cover and decorate with cream just before serving.

Raspberry Tipsy Gâteau

Mrs Ann Kinchin, from Plymouth in Devon, made this gâteau when she was a finalist in one of the Cook of the Year competitions.

For 4 to 6 portions

METRIC	IMPERIAL
2 eggs	2 eggs
Castor sugar	Castor sugar
50g plain flour	2oz plain flour
1 × 2.5ml spoon baking powder	½ level teaspoon baking powder
1 small (213g) can raspberries	1 small (7½oz) can raspberries
4 × 15ml spoons sherry	4 tablespoons sherry
4 × 15ml spoons single cream	4 tablespoons single cream
150ml double cream	5 fluid oz double cream
4 angelica leaves	4 angelica leaves
4 walnut halves	4 walnut halves

1. Prepare a moderately hot oven (200 deg C, 400 deg F, Gas Mark 6). Brush a 1 litre (2 pint) fluted ring mould with oil.
2. Bring a large saucepan of water to boil; remove from heat. Place eggs and 50g (2oz) castor sugar in a basin over saucepan; whisk until mixture becomes thick and leaves a trail when whisk is lifted. Remove bowl from saucepan; continue whisking until mixture is cool.
3. Sift flour and baking powder together; carefully fold into egg mixture with a metal spoon.
4. Pour into prepared mould and shake mould gently, to level mixture. Bake on shelf just below centre of oven for 15 to 25 minutes. Test by pressing with fingers. If cooked, sponge should spring back and have begun to shrink from sides of mould. Leave to cool in mould for 5 minutes, then remove sponge from mould and leave to cool completely on a wire rack.
5. Drain syrup from can of raspberries. Mix 4 × 15ml spoons (4 tablespoons) syrup with sherry in a small bowl. Place sponge on a serving dish, then spoon the sherry mixture over it.
6. Place single and double creams together in a basin with 1 × 15ml spoon (1 level tablespoon) castor sugar; whisk until just stiff. Using a round-ended knife, spread cream over cake, covering completely.
7. Dry raspberries on kitchen paper; arrange 4 groups of 3 raspberries on top of gâteau; place an angelica leaf with each group. Arrange remaining raspberries around bottom edge of gâteau. Place a walnut half between each raspberry cluster on top. Keep gâteau in refrigerator.

Almond Fruit Shortcake

Mrs Pamela Hutton, from Spennymoor in Co Durham, cooked this peachy dessert which has a lattice-work look.

For 6 portions

METRIC	IMPERIAL
PASTRY	PASTRY
150g soft margarine, chilled	6oz soft margarine, chilled
50g castor sugar	2oz castor sugar
50g ground almonds	2oz ground almonds
Lemon juice	Lemon juice
3 drops almond essence	3 drops almond essence
200g plain flour	8oz plain flour
FILLING	FILLING
1 large (425g) can sliced peaches	1 large (15oz) can sliced peaches
1 × 10ml spoon cornflour	2 level teaspoons cornflour
1 × 15ml spoon top of the milk	1 tablespoon top of the milk
Icing sugar	Icing sugar

1. Prepare a moderate oven (190 deg C, 375 deg F, Gas Mark 5). Place a 20cm (8in) fluted flan ring on a baking sheet.
2. Place chilled margarine sugar, almonds, 1 × 5ml spoon (1 teaspoon) lemon juice, almond essence and 4 × 15ml spoons (2 rounded tablespoons) of the flour in a large bowl. Beat together until soft. Stir in the remaining flour; mix to form a soft dough. Turn the dough out on to a floured board and knead lightly.
3. Cut off one third of dough; reserve for lattice. Press remaining pastry over base and up side of flan ring, pressing into flutes with the fingers. Prick base all over with a fork; leave in a cool place while preparing filling.
4. To make filling: drain syrup thoroughly from peaches. Place peaches, 1 × 15ml spoon (1 tablespoon) syrup and 1 × 15ml spoon (1 tablespoon) lemon juice in a small saucepan. Bring to boil, cover with a lid and simmer for 10 to 15 minutes until peaches are very soft. Beat until smooth. Blend cornflour with top of the milk; stir into peach mixture and bring to boil, stirring. Cook gently for 2 minutes. Remove saucepan from heat and leave filling to cool.
5. Roll out remaining pastry to an 18cm (7in) by 8cm (4in) oblong; cut into 8, 1cm (½in) wide strips. Spread the filling in flan. Place 4 pastry strips over filling; place remaining 4 diagonally across, to form a lattice. Press strips on to pastry edge and trim, if necessary. Bake in centre of oven for 25 to 30 minutes, until lightly browned. Cool, dust with icing sugar; serve with cream.

73

Pineapple Wheels

Mrs Dorothy Sleightholme, from Pickering, North Yorkshire, gave us this recipe, which is the ideal dessert for a dinner party.

For 4 portions

METRIC	IMPERIAL
25g pistachio nuts	1oz pistachio nuts
1 large (425g) can pineapple rings	1 large (15½oz) can pineapple rings
1 × 15ml spoon kirsch liqueur	1 tablespoon kirsch liqueur
25g (or 1 envelope) gelatine	½oz (or 1 envelope) gelatine
2 eggs	2 eggs
50g castor sugar	2oz castor sugar
150ml double cream	5 fluid oz double cream
Angelica	Angelica
4 maraschino cherries	4 maraschino cherries

1. Place nuts in a small bowl; cover with boiling water. Leave for 1 minute; drain and remove skins (see note).
2. Drain syrup from can of pineapple; reserve. Place pineapple rings in a bowl; sprinkle with kirsch.
3. Measure 3 × 15ml spoons (3 tablespoons) pineapple syrup into a small basin; add gelatine. Place basin in a saucepan of water over a moderate heat; stir until the gelatine has dissolved.
4. Separate eggs; place whites in a clean, grease-free bowl and yolks in a small basin. Add sugar to yolks and whisk together until thick. Heat 125ml (¼ pint) of remaining pineapple syrup in a small saucepan; bring to boil. Whisk it into egg yolk mixture with the dissolved gelatine.
5. Reserve 4 pineapple rings for decoration; chop remainder and add to syrup mixture with kirsch from bowl. Leave in a cool place until mixture is just beginning to thicken.
6. Whisk egg whites until stiff, but not dry. Place cream in a basin; whip lightly. Reserve 1 generous 15ml spoon (tablespoon) cream for decoration; fold remainder into gelatine mixture, with egg whites. Divide mixture between 4 individual sundae glasses; leave in a cool place to set.
7. Chop nuts finely. Cut each pineapple ring into 8 sections. Dip outside edge of each section in chopped nuts; arrange 8 pineapple sections around edge of each glass. Place a thin strip of angelica between each section. Place a little of the reserved cream in centre of each glass; top each with a cherry.
Note: if pistachio nuts are not available, finely chop 25g (1oz) blanched almonds and place them in a small, screw-topped jar, adding 3 drops green food colouring. Shake the jar until the almonds are evenly coloured.

Coffee Savarin Japonnaise

(pictured opposite)

Mrs Mary Hamlin, from Abingdon, Oxfordshire, won first prize with this dessert in one of the Cook of the Year competitions.

For 6 to 8 portions

METRIC	IMPERIAL
SAVARIN	SAVARIN
1 × 5ml spoon instant coffee	1 level teaspoon instant coffee
1 × 2.5ml spoon castor sugar	½ level teaspoon castor sugar
Boiling water	Boiling water
75g plain flour	2½oz plain flour
A pinch of salt	A pinch of salt
25g margarine	1oz margarine
15g fresh yeast	¼oz fresh yeast
1 egg	1 egg
JAPONNAISE	JAPONNAISE
2 egg whites	2 egg whites
100g castor sugar	4oz castor sugar
75g ground almonds	3oz ground almonds
SYRUP	SYRUP
75g granulated sugar	3oz granulated sugar
125ml sweet sherry	4 fluid oz sweet sherry
COFFEE ICING	COFFEE ICING
1 × 5ml spoon instant coffee	1 level teaspoon instant coffee
Boiling water	Boiling water
100g icing sugar	4oz icing sugar
50g margarine	2oz margarine
DECORATION	DECORATION
150ml double cream	5 fluid oz double cream
2 × 15ml spoons milk	2 tablespoons milk
3 glacé cherries	3 glacé cherries
15 angelica leaves	15 angelica leaves

1. Dissolve 1 × 5ml spoon (1 level teaspoon) instant coffee and 1 × 2.5ml spoon (½ level teaspoon) sugar in 2 × 15ml spoons (2 tablespoons) boiling water; leave until lukewarm.
2. Place flour and salt in a bowl; add 25g (1oz) margarine, cut into small pieces.
3. Add yeast to coffee mixture; stir until dissolved.
4. Make a well in centre of flour; add yeast mixture. Sprinkle yeast mixture with a little flour from side of bowl. Leave in a warm place for 15 to 20 minutes, or until yeast starts to froth.
5. Prepare a moderately hot oven (200 deg C, 400 deg F, Gas Mark 6). Grease an 18cm (7in) round sandwich tin. Line with greaseproof paper; grease paper.
6. Add egg to yeast mixture; beat well with a wooden

spoon for 2 to 3 minutes, until mixture is of a smooth batter consistency.

7. Pour mixture into prepared tin; level top with the back of a metal spoon. Cover with greased polythene or foil and leave in a warm place until risen to top of tin.

8. Remove polythene or foil and bake in centre of oven for 15 to 20 minutes. Test by pressing with the fingers. If cooked, savarin should spring back and have begun to shrink from side of tin. Turn out, remove paper and leave to cool on a wire rack. Reduce oven temperature to cool (170 deg C, 325 deg F, Gas Mark 3).

9. Meanwhile, make japonnaise: line 2 baking sheets with silicone-treated paper. Draw a 20cm (8in) circle on each piece of paper, using sandwich tin as a guide.

10. Place egg whites in a clean, grease-free bowl. Whisk until stiff, but not dry. Whisk in half the sugar, then fold in remainder, with the ground almonds, using a metal spoon, until all the sugar and almonds have been incorporated. Divide mixture between the 2 circles and spread inside marked lines with a palette knife.

11. Bake in centre of oven for 30 to 35 minutes, when japonnaise should be lightly browned and firm. After 15 minutes' cooking time, lightly mark on top of each japonnaise an 18cm (7in) circle, using sandwich tin as a guide.

12. Leave to cool on baking sheets for 20 minutes, then remove paper. Trim each japonnaise to 18cm (7in) marked circle. Place trimmings between 2 sheets of greaseproof paper; crush trimmings with a rolling pin.

13. To make syrup: place granulated sugar and 50ml (2 fluid oz) water in a medium-sized saucepan. Heat gently until sugar has dissolved; leave to cool, then add sherry.

14. Place savarin on a wire rack over a plate. Spoon syrup over savarin; leave for 10 minutes. Spoon remaining syrup from plate over savarin, until all the syrup has been absorbed.

15. To make coffee icing: dissolve 1 × 5ml spoon (1 level teaspoon) instant coffee in 1 × 10ml spoon (2 teaspoons) boiling water; leave until cold. Sift icing sugar into a bowl; add 50g (2oz) margarine and coffee. Beat with a wooden spoon until light and fluffy.

16. Divide icing into 3 equal portions; spread the underside of each japonnaise layer with a portion of icing. Sandwich the syrup-soaked savarin in between the 2 layers, iced sides inside. Spread remaining icing evenly around side; coat in the crushed japonnaise crumbs. Place on a serving plate.

17. Place cream and milk in a basin; whisk until just thick. Spread top of japonnaise with half the cream; place remainder in a nylon piping bag, fitted with a small star tube. Pipe a lattice pattern across top. Pipe stars around edge. Decorate with cherries and angelica.

COFFEE SAVARIN JAPONNAISE

75

Chilled Citrus Cheesecake

(pictured on page 80)

Mrs Barbara Vaz, from Pinner in Middlesex, enjoys making this unusually tasty cheesecake.

For 6 to 8 portions

METRIC	IMPERIAL
6 digestive biscuits	6 digestive biscuits
75g butter	3oz butter
125g castor sugar	5oz castor sugar
2 medium-sized oranges	2 medium-sized oranges
1 small lemon	1 small lemon
300g curd cheese	¾lb curd cheese
150ml single cream	5 fluid oz single cream
25g (or 2 envelopes) gelatine	1oz (or 2 envelopes) gelatine
3 eggs	3 eggs
150ml double cream	5 fluid oz double cream

DECORATION	DECORATION
1 gold-coloured doily	1 gold-coloured doily
1 metre (4cm wide) red ribbon	1yd (1½in wide) red ribbon

APRICOT SAUCE	APRICOT SAUCE
6 × 15ml spoons apricot jam	6 level tablespoons apricot jam
1 × 10ml spoon lemon juice	2 teaspoons lemon juice

1. Lightly brush a 20cm (8in) round cake tin (preferably with a removeable base) with melted fat. Line side and base of tin with 1 layer of foil.
2. Crush biscuits with a rolling pin between 2 sheets of greaseproof paper. Place the butter in a small saucepan and heat until melted. Remove from heat; stir in biscuit crumbs and 50g (2oz) castor sugar. Mix well; leave to cool in saucepan.
3. Scrub oranges and lemon; grate rinds into a basin. Add curd cheese and single cream; mix well.
4. Squeeze juice from oranges and lemon; pour through a sieve into a large bowl and add gelatine. Place bowl over a saucepan of water over a moderate heat and stir until gelatine has dissolved.
5. Separate eggs; place whites in a clean, grease-free bowl. Place yolks and 75g (3oz) castor sugar in bowl with gelatine mixture. Mix well and heat gently, stirring occasionally, for 15 to 20 minutes, or until mixture has thickened slightly and will coat the back of a spoon.
6. Remove bowl from top of saucepan and immediately stir in curd cheese mixture; mix until smooth.
7. Whisk egg whites until stiff, but not dry. Whisk double cream until it just holds its shape. Using a metal spoon, fold egg whites, then cream, into cheese mixture. Pour mixture into prepared tin.
8. Crumble and sprinkle biscuit crumb mixture evenly over top of cheesecake; press lightly with back of a spoon. Leave in a cool place to set.
9. To serve: invert tin on to a serving dish; gently remove foil. Decorate top of cheesecake with a cut-out shape from gold doily. Cut a length of greaseproof paper, about 71cm (28in) long and 4cm (1½in) wide. Line ribbon with greaseproof paper strip; place around cake, paper on the inside. Secure ends with a pin.
10. To make sauce: place jam in a small saucepan. Add 3 × 15ml spoons (3 tablespoons) water and the lemon juice; heat gently and bring to boil, stirring.
11. Sieve sauce into a small basin. Reheat sauce and serve hot with the cheesecake.

Chocolate Rum Garland

Mrs Jill Ronson, from Ormskirk in Lancashire, uses rose leaves to add the finishing touch to this recipe.

For 4 portions

METRIC	IMPERIAL
3 eggs	3 eggs
100g castor sugar	3½oz castor sugar
2 × 15ml spoons oil	2 tablespoons oil
75g plain flour	3oz plain flour

FILLING	FILLING
100g plain chocolate	4oz plain chocolate
2 eggs yolks	2 egg yolks
50g castor sugar	2oz castor sugar
Vanilla essence	Vanilla essence
2 × 10ml spoons cornflour	1 rounded dessertspoon cornflour
250ml milk	½ pint milk

50g plain chocolate	2oz plain chocolate
Rose leaves	Rose leaves
Dark rum	Dark rum
150ml double cream	5 fluid oz double cream
2 × 15ml spoons single cream	2 tablespoons single cream
1 egg white	1 egg white

1. Prepare a moderate oven (190 deg C, 375 deg F, Gas Mark 5). Grease and flour a ¾ litre (1½ pint) ring mould.
2. Separate eggs; place whites in a clean, grease-free bowl and yolks and 100g (3½oz) castor sugar in another clean bowl.
3. Whisk egg whites until stiff, but not dry.
4. Whisk egg yolks and sugar together until mixture becomes thick and leaves a trail when whisk is lifted. Whisk in 1 × 15ml spoon (1 tablespoon) oil.
5. Sift half the flour into egg yolk mixture; fold in with a metal spoon. Fold in egg whites. Sift remaining flour into mixture and fold in, with remaining 1 × 15ml spoon (1 tablespoon) oil.
6. Pour into prepared mould; bake in centre of oven for

76

15 to 25 minutes. Test by pressing with the fingers. If cooked, sponge should spring back and have begun to shrink from the side of the mould.

7. Leave to cool in tin for 5 minutes, then remove from mould and leave to cool completely on a wire rack.

8. To make filling: place 100g (4oz) chocolate in a dry basin over a small saucepan of hot, but not boiling, water; stir occasionally until melted.

9. Cream egg yolks, 50g (2oz) castor sugar, a few drops vanilla essence and cornflour together in a basin. Beat in melted chocolate and milk. Pour into a saucepan; bring slowly to boil and cook for 1 minute, stirring continuously. Remove from heat; place in basin and cover with a piece of wetted greaseproof paper, to prevent a skin forming. Leave to cool, then place in refrigerator.

10. To make chocolate leaves: place 50g (2oz) chocolate in a basin over a small saucepan of hot, but not boiling, water; stir occasionally until melted.

11. Wash and dry 8 medium-sized and 8 small rose leaves, with stalks. Draw underside of leaves over surface of chocolate. Drain off excess chocolate and place leaves, chocolate sides uppermost, on greaseproof paper. Leave in refrigerator for 30 minutes, to set.

12. Place sponge ring on a serving plate. Beat 1 × 15ml spoon (1 tablespoon) rum into filling.

13. Place filling in centre of sponge; spread to within 1cm (½in) of top edge.

14. Place double and single cream, 1 × 15ml spoon (1 tablespoon) rum and egg white in a bowl and whisk until thick.

15. Spread 2 × 15ml spoons (2 tablespoons) cream over top and side of sponge. Place remaining cream in a piping bag, fitted with a large star tube. Pipe stars around top and bottom edges and middle of sponge.

16. Carefully peel off rose leaves from chocolate. Place small chocolate leaves around top edge of sponge and medium leaves around bottom. Keep in refrigerator.

Pineapple Poll

(pictured on back cover)

Miss Jane Slocombe, from Lordshill, Southampton, sent us this delicious recipe for mincemeat shortcake, topped with pineapple.

For 6 portions

METRIC	IMPERIAL
SHORTCAKE	SHORTCAKE
150g self-raising flour	**6oz self-raising flour**
Pinch of salt	**Pinch of salt**
75g butter	**3oz butter**
50g castor sugar	**2oz castor sugar**
1 egg	**1 egg**
100g mincemeat	**4oz mincemeat**
1 small (226g) can pineapple slices	**1 small (8oz) can pineapple slices**
125ml double cream	**4 fluid oz double cream**
2 glacé cherries	**2 glacé cherries**

1. Prepare a moderate oven (190 deg C, 375 deg F, Gas Mark 5). Place a 23cm (9in) loose-based, fluted flan tin on a baking sheet.

2. Place flour and salt in a bowl. Add butter, cut into small pieces and rub in with the fingertips until mixture resembles fine breadcrumbs. Add sugar and mix.

3. Beat egg and add to bowl. Mix with a fork, to form a soft dough. Turn out dough on to a floured board and knead lightly; roll out to a circle, 4cm (1½in) larger all round than flan ring. Support dough on rolling pin and lift into tin. Press dough with floured fingertips up side of tin, to form an edge.

4. Spread mincemeat over dough. Bake in centre of oven for 15 to 20 minutes, until shortcake is risen and golden brown. Leave to cool in tin. Remove from tin, when cold, and place on a serving plate.

5. To decorate: drain syrup from can of pineapple slices. Arrange the 4 slices in shortcake case.

6. Place cream in a basin and whisk until it just holds its shape. Place in a nylon piping bag fitted with a large star tube. Pipe a swirl of cream in centre of each pineapple slice and large stars around edge of shortcake case.

7. Cut each glacé cherry in half. Place 1 half on top of each swirl of cream. Keep in refrigerator until needed.

Breadcrumb Pudding

Mrs Elizabeth Anderson, a reader from Southfields in London, often serves this easy-to-make economical pudding to her husband.

For 4 portions

METRIC	IMPERIAL
250ml milk	**½ pint milk**
25g butter	**½oz butter**
50g fresh white breadcrumbs	**2oz fresh white breadcrumbs**
150g castor sugar	**5½oz castor sugar**
2 eggs	**2 eggs**
3 × 15ml spoons raspberry jam	**3 level tablespoons raspberry jam**

1. Prepare a moderate oven (190 deg C, 375 deg F, Gas Mark 5). Grease a ½ litre (1 pint) pie dish.

2. Heat milk and butter in a saucepan. Add breadcrumbs and cook for a few minutes. Stir in 50g (1½oz) of sugar and remove from heat.

3. Separate eggs; place whites in a clean, grease-free bowl and stir yolks into breadcrumb mixture. Place in pie dish. Bake in centre of oven for 20 minutes, until mixture is set.

4. Remove from oven and spread with raspberry jam.

5. Whisk egg whites until stiff, but not dry; add half the remaining sugar and whisk until stiff again. Fold in remainder of sugar with a metal spoon.

6. Pile meringue on top of jam; return the pie dish to the oven and cook for a further 5 to 10 minutes, until the tips of the meringue are golden brown.

*Informal parties
should be relaxing and enjoyable for
everyone, including the hostess; so plan your menu as a buffet –
most of the following recipes can be made in advance and will keep well*

Red and Golden Kofta Pilau

(pictured on page 80)

*Mrs Barbara Vaz, of Pinner, Middlesex, came third in
one of our Cook of the Year competitions with this recipe.*

For 4 portions

METRIC	IMPERIAL
KEBABS	KEBABS
¾kg blade end shoulder of lamb	1½lb blade and shoulder of lamb
Sprig of parsley	Sprig of parsley
1 clove of garlic	1 clove of garlic
1 medium-sized onion	1 medium-sized onion
1 × 5ml spoon salt	1 level teaspoon salt
½ × 2.5ml spoon pepper	¼ level teaspoon pepper
1 × 5ml spoon cinnamon	1 level teaspoon cinnamon
Juice of half a lemon	Juice of half a lemon
2 × 15ml spoons fresh white breadcrumbs	1 rounded tablespoon fresh white breadcrumbs
1 egg yolk	1 egg yolk
1 beef stock cube	1 beef stock cube
250ml boiling water	½ pint boiling water
TOMATO AND PINEAPPLE SAUCE	TOMATO AND PINEAPPLE SAUCE
1 medium-sized onion	1 medium-sized onion
25g butter	1oz butter
1 × 10ml spoon oil	2 teaspoons oil
1 × 10ml spoon paprika	2 level teaspoons paprika
1 small (226g) can tomatoes	1 small (8oz) can tomatoes
1 small (240g) can sliced pineapple	1 small (8½oz) can sliced pineapple
Juice of half a lemon	Juice of half a lemon
1 × 5ml spoon castor sugar	1 level teaspoon castor sugar
1 × 2.5ml spoon salt	½ level teaspoon salt
Pepper	Pepper
PILAU	PILAU
2 medium-sized onions	2 medium-sized onions
50g butter	2oz butter
1 × 15ml spoon oil	1 tablespoon oil
1 × 5ml spoon turmeric	1 level teaspoon turmeric
1 × 5ml spoon cinnamon	1 level teaspoon cinnamon
½kg long-grain rice	1lb long-grain rice
3 chicken stock cubes	3 chicken stock cubes
1 litre boiling water	2 pints boiling water
1 × 10ml spoon salt	2 level teaspoons salt
100g frozen peas	4oz frozen peas
100g sultanas	4oz sultanas
GARNISH	GARNISH
2 hard-boiled eggs	2 hard-boiled eggs
2 medium-sized tomatoes	2 medium-sized tomatoes
Sprig of parsley	Sprig of parsley
Half a carton of natural yoghourt	Half a carton of natural yoghourt

1. Remove skin and excess fat from meat; cut meat into long strips. Wash and dry parsley. Peel garlic and onion; cut onion into quarters. Coarsely mince meat, parsley, garlic and onion 3 times. Place in bowl; add salt, pepper, cinnamon, lemon juice, breadcrumbs and egg yolk. Crumble beef stock cube and add to boiling water; stir until dissolved, then add 1 × 15ml spoon (1 tablespoon) stock to meat mixture and mix well. Divide into 16 and roll each portion into a sausage shape; thread on to 4 skewers.

2. To make sauce: peel and chop onion; fry in a small saucepan in butter and oil, mixed, for 5 minutes. Stir in paprika, contents of can of tomatoes, remaining stock, drained syrup from can of pineapple, lemon juice, sugar, salt and shake of pepper. Cook slowly, uncovered, for 30 minutes; sieve and return to pan. Chop 1 slice of pineapple; add to pan; reserve remainder for garnish.

3. To make pilau: peel and slice onions. Heat butter and oil in a large saucepan; fry onion gently for 5 minutes. Add turmeric, cinnamon, rice, stock cubes, boiling water and salt. Stir well and cook gently for 15 minutes, uncovered; add peas and sultanas. Cook for a further 10 minutes, until liquid is absorbed and rice is cooked. Test by pressing a grain between thumb and finger; if rice is not cooked, add more water and continue cooking.

4. While rice is cooking, prepare a hot grill. Place kebabs on grill rack and cook for 10 to 15 minutes, turning frequently. Reheat sauce.

5. To serve: pile rice on to a large, warmed serving dish. Arrange 2 kebabs at each side of dish on rice. Place alternate slices of hard-boiled egg and tomato in centre of rice, between kebabs. Cut each remaining pineapple slice into 4 sections; arrange sections at each side of line of egg and tomato. Garnish centre with parsley. Pour hot sauce into a warmed serving bowl. Mix yoghourt, in carton, until smooth; lightly stir into sauce.

Kidneys in Sherry Sauce

Mrs Frances Dennison, from St Leonards-on-Sea, Sussex, was a finalist in one of our Cook of the Year competitions.

For 4 portions

METRIC	IMPERIAL
8 lambs' kidneys	8 lambs' kidneys
1 large onion	1 large onion
100g button mushrooms	4oz button mushrooms
4 medium-sized tomatoes	4 medium-sized tomatoes
1 clove of garlic	1 clove of garlic
Salt	Salt
50g butter	2oz butter
2 × 15ml spoons plain flour	2 level tablespoons plain flour
1 × 15ml spoon tomato purée	1 level tablespoon tomato purée
4 × 15ml spoons sweet sherry	4 tablespoons sweet sherry
1 beef stock cube	1 beef stock cube
1 bay leaf	1 bay leaf
Pepper	Pepper
1 (12mg) packet powdered saffron	1 (1.9 grains) packet powdered saffron
200g long-grain rice	8oz long-grain rice
Watercress	Watercress

1. Skin kidneys; cut in halves, remove the cores. Peel and slice onion; wash and slice mushrooms. Place tomatoes in a basin and cover with boiling water. Leave for 1 minute; drain, then peel, halve and remove seeds. Discard seeds and cut tomato shells into strips.
2. Peel clove of garlic and place on a saucer with 1 × 5ml spoon (1 level teaspoon) salt. Using a round-ended knife, rub salt against garlic to crush clove.
3. Melt butter in a frying pan; add kidneys. Fry gently for 5 minutes, stirring occasionally. Remove kidneys from pan and place on a plate; cover and put to one side. Gently fry sliced onion in fat remaining in pan for 5 minutes; add sliced mushrooms and cook for a further 3 to 4 minutes.
4. Stir in flour, tomato purée, sherry and 250ml (½ pint) water; crumble and add stock cube, with garlic, bay leaf and kidneys. Bring to boil, stirring. Cover pan with foil; simmer gently for 20 minutes. Add tomato strips and continue cooking for a further 5 minutes. Taste and season with salt and pepper. Remove bay leaf.
5. Bring a large saucepan of water to boil. Add saffron and some salt. Add rice and boil, uncovered, for about 12 minutes. Test by pressing a grain between thumb and finger. Drain in a sieve or colander; rinse with hot water. Arrange rice around edge of a warmed dish. Pour kidney mixture in centre. Garnish with sprigs of watercress.

Salami and Cheese Flan

Mrs Joyce Fry, from Bruton in Somerset, sent us this long-time favourite recipe.

For 4 to 6 portions

METRIC	IMPERIAL
SHORTCRUST PASTRY	SHORTCRUST PASTRY
150g plain flour	6oz plain flour
1 × 2.5ml spoon salt	½ level teaspoon salt
75g mixed cooking fats	3oz mixed cooking fats
Cold water to mix	Cold water to mix
FILLING	FILLING
100g salami, sliced	4oz salami, sliced
2 eggs	2 eggs
125ml milk	¼ pint milk
1 × 5ml spoon mixed dried herbs	1 level teaspoon mixed dried herbs
Pepper	Pepper
100g cottage cheese	4oz cottage cheese
Sprig of parsley to garnish	Sprig of parsley to garnish

1. Prepare a moderate oven (180 deg C, 350 deg F, Gas Mark 4). Place a 20cm (8in) plain flan ring on a baking sheet. Place flour and salt in a bowl. Add fats, cut into small pieces and rub in with the fingertips until mixture resembles fine breadcrumbs. Add about 1 × 15ml spoon (1 tablespoon water) and mix with a fork to form a firm dough.
2. Turn out on to a floured board and knead lightly. Roll out to a circle, about 4cm (1½in) larger all around than flan ring. Support pastry on rolling pin and lift on to flan ring on baking sheet.
3. Gently ease pastry into flan ring. Roll off surplus pastry with a rolling pin across top of flan ring. Prick all over with a fork; leave in refrigerator while making the filling.
4. Reserve 4 slices of salami for garnish; arrange remainder over base of flan.
5. Place eggs, milk, herbs and a shake of pepper in a bowl; beat together. Stir in cottage cheese. Pour mixture into flan case and bake just above centre of oven for 40 to 50 minutes, until pastry is cooked and filling is firm.
6. Remove flan ring; place flan on a serving dish. Cut reserved salami slices into quarters; arrange around edge of flan and in a circle in centre. Garnish with a sprig of parsley in centre. Serve the flan hot or cold with a salad or boiled potatoes and a green vegetable.

RED AND GOLDEN KOFTA PILAU (FOREGROUND) AND CHILLED CITRUS CHEESECAKE *Recipes on pages 76 and 78*

Orange Blossom Baskets

(pictured below)

Mrs Gloria Heane, from Market Harborough in Leicestershire, won third prize with this recipe in one of our Cook of the Year competitions.

For 4 portions

METRIC	IMPERIAL
3 medium-sized oranges	**3 medium-sized oranges**
1 medium-sized lemon	**1 medium-sized lemon**
Castor sugar	**Castor sugar**
2 × 15ml spoons **cornflour**	**2 level tablespoons** **cornflour**
1 egg	**1 egg**
1 × 10ml spoon sweet **sherry**	**1 dessertspoon sweet** **sherry**
150ml double cream	**5 fluid oz double cream**
150ml single cream	**5 fluid oz single cream**
Orange food colouring	**Orange food colouring**
DECORATION	DECORATION
Evergreen leaves or **angelica leaves**	**Evergreen leaves or** **angelica leaves**

1. Scrub fruit. Cut 1 orange in half; from each half cut a thin slice. Remove flesh and white pith from each slice; cut circles of rind in halves, to form 4 handles. Chop the flesh cut from the orange slices and place in a saucepan.

2. Cut remaining oranges in halves. Scrape out flesh with a teaspoon, discarding pith and pips; place in saucepan. Scrape pith from orange cups; reserve cups.

3. Grate rind from first orange and rind from half the lemon; add to saucepan, with 75g (2½ oz) castor sugar. Squeeze juice from orange and one half of lemon; blend together, with cornflour, in a basin. Add to saucepan.

4. Separate egg; place white in a clean, grease-free bowl and yolk in saucepan. Add sherry to saucepan. Bring to boil, stirring continuously; cook over a low heat for 2 minutes. Leave sauce until quite cold.

5. Place double and single cream in a bowl; whisk until just thick. Whisk egg white until stiff, but not dry. Add egg white and half the cream to sauce; fold in with a metal spoon, until all the cream and egg white have been incorporated. Fill each orange cup with mixture; place remaining mixture into small glasses.

6. Add 1 × 5ml spoon (1 teaspoon) of sugar to remaining cream. Fit a piping bag with a No 5 star tube; lay bag on the table. Place half the cream inside bag, so that it lies on bottom of bag.

7. Colour remaining cream orange with a little food colouring. Place orange cream inside bag on top of the plain cream.

8. Pipe orange and white stars of cream over mixture in orange cups and glasses (reserve mixture in glasses, in refrigerator, for another meal).

9. Place orange cups on glass dishes. Decorate dishes with evergreen leaves and place orange handles in position, to form baskets. If using angelica leaves, arrange about 6 around top edge of each orange basket.

ORANGE BLOSSOM BASKETS

81

Stuffed Eggs

Mrs Elizabeth Brown, from Hammersmith, London, finds this a very quick-to-make buffet party dish.

For 6 portions

METRIC	IMPERIAL
6 eggs	6 eggs
1 (53g) jar shrimp and salmon paste	1 (1⅞oz) jar shrimp and salmon paste
1 × 15ml spoon salad cream	1 level tablespoon salad cream
1 × 2.5ml spoon salt	½ level teaspoon salt
Pepper	Pepper
1 small gherkin	1 small gherkin
1 small lettuce	1 small lettuce

1. Hard boil eggs for 10 minutes; crack and leave to cool in cold water. Shell and dry on kitchen paper.
2. Cut eggs in halves lengthwise; carefully remove yolks and place in a basin. Add shrimp and salmon paste, salad cream, 1 × 2.5ml (½ level teaspoon) salt and a shake of pepper.
3. Beat together until smooth; taste and add more salt and pepper, if necessary. Place mixture in a large piping bag, fitted with a large star tube; pipe swirls of mixture back into each egg white.
4. Cut gherkin into 12 slices; top each egg with a slice.
5. Remove and discard outer leaves from lettuce; wash lettuce and drain well. Arrange leaves on a large plate; place egg halves on top. Chill until ready to serve.

Sauté of Liver in Red Wine Sauce

Mrs Andrea Hutchinson, from Lower Somersham in Suffolk, entered one of our Cook of the Year competitions with this tasty recipe.

For 4 portions

METRIC	IMPERIAL
1 large onion	1 large onion
1 small green pepper	1 small green pepper
100g button mushrooms	4oz button mushrooms
300g ox liver	12oz ox liver
Plain flour	Plain flour
Salt and pepper	Salt and pepper
100g streaky bacon	4oz streaky bacon
1 beef stock cube	1 beef stock cube
250ml boiling water	½ pint boiling water
125ml red wine	4 fluid oz red wine
25g butter	1oz butter
3 × 15ml spoons oil	3 tablespoons oil

1. Peel and thinly slice onion. Cut pepper in half lengthwise; discard seeds, core and white pith. Slice the green pepper finely. Wash and slice the mushrooms.
2. Trim liver and cut into thin, 5cm (2in) long strips. Mix 2 × 15ml spoons (1 rounded tablespoon) flour and a little salt and pepper together on a plate; turn liver in seasoned flour, to coat. Remove rind and bone from bacon; cut bacon lengthwise into 2cm by 5cm (¾in by 2in) strips.
3. Dissolve stock cube in 250ml (½ pint) boiling water and add red wine.
4. Melt butter in a large frying pan then add 2 × 15ml spoons (2 tablespoons) oil and heat. Add coated liver and gently fry for 20 minutes, stirring occasionally. Remove from pan; place on a plate and keep warm. Add 1 × 15ml spoon (1 tablespoon) oil to frying pan and heat. Add bacon, onion, mushrooms and green pepper; fry gently for 10 minutes.
5. Return liver to frying pan. Stir in 1 × 15ml spoon (1 level tablespoon) flour and cook for 1 minute.
6. Stir in stock and wine mixture; bring to boil, stirring, and cook for 10 minutes. Taste and season with salt and pepper, if necessary. Serve with fluffy boiled rice.

Party Pizza

Mrs P Masters, from Stanford-le-Hope in Essex, serves this pizza, either hot or cold, with a variety of salads.

For 4 to 6 portions

METRIC	IMPERIAL
200g self-raising flour	8oz self-raising flour
1 × 5ml spoon baking powder	1 level teaspoon baking powder
1 × 2.5ml spoon salt	½ level teaspoon salt
1 × 2.5ml spoon oregano	½ level teaspoon oregano
50g margarine	2oz margarine
6 × 15ml spoons milk	6 tablespoons milk
TOPPING	TOPPING
1 small (225g) can tomatoes	1 small (8oz) can tomatoes
Garlic salt	Garlic salt
Oregano	Oregano
100g Cheddar cheese	4oz Cheddar cheese
1 (124g) can sardines in oil	1 (4⅜oz) can sardines in oil
4 rashers streaky bacon	4 rashers streaky bacon

1. Prepare a moderate oven (190 deg C, 375 deg F, Gas Mark 5). Grease a baking sheet.
2. Sift flour, baking powder, 1 × 2.5ml spoon (½ level teaspoon) salt and 1 × 2.5ml spoon (½ level teaspoon) oregano into a bowl. Add margarine, cut into small pieces and rub in with the fingertips until the mixture resembles fine breadcrumbs.
3. Add milk, all at once, and mix with a fork to form a soft dough. Turn out on to a floured board and knead lightly with the fingertips.
4. Roll out dough to a 25cm (10in) round; gently lift on to baking sheet.
5. Drain tomatoes thoroughly in a sieve; spread over

dough. Sprinkle a little garlic salt and oregano over tomatoes.

6. Grate cheese; sprinkle evenly over tomatoes. Drain sardines; cut each sardine in half lengthwise and remove bones. Remove rind and bone from bacon; cut each rasher in half across length. Arrange sardines and bacon alternately on top of cheese, so that sardines and bacon overlap, to form a circle.

7. Bake on shelf just above centre of oven for 25 to 35 minutes, until pizza is golden and topping is cooked.

Austrian Apple Strudel

Mrs Rene Manhine, who comes from London, sent us this, one of her favourite recipes.

For 6 to 8 portions

METRIC	IMPERIAL
PASTRY	PASTRY
350g self-raising flour	**12oz self-raising flour**
175g margarine	**6oz margarine**
Cold water to mix	**Cold water to mix.**
FILLING	FILLING
2 medium-sized cooking apples	**2 medium-sized cooking apples**
50g blanched almonds	**2oz blanched almonds**
50g dates	**2oz dates**
75g raisins	**3oz raisins**
4 × 15ml spoons castor sugar	**2 rounded tablespoons castor sugar**
1 × 5ml spoon ground cinnamon	**1 level teaspoon ground cinnamon**
Icing sugar	**Icing sugar**

1. Prepare a moderate oven (190 deg C, 375 deg F, Gas Mark 5).

2. Place flour in a bowl. Add margarine, cut into small pieces and rub in with the fingertips until mixture resembles fine breadcrumbs.

3. Add about 3 × 15ml spoons (3 tablespoons) water and mix with a fork to form a firm dough.

4. Turn out dough on to a floured board and knead lightly. Roll out pastry to a 38cm (15in) square.

5. Peel, core and slice apples. Spread evenly on pastry, leaving a 2.5cm (1in) border all around. Chop almonds and dates; spread over apples with raisins. Sprinkle sugar and cinnamon over filling.

6. Brush edges of pastry with water, fold borders on 2 opposite sides over filling, then roll up, Swiss-roll fashion.

7. Wrap loosely in foil and place on a baking sheet. Bake in centre of oven for 1 hour. Open foil, fold back to expose roll and cook for a further 20 to 30 minutes.

8. Lift out of foil and leave to cool on a wire rack. To serve, dredge with icing sugar; cut into 5cm (2in) pieces.

Chocolate Gâteau

Mrs Valerie Henderson, a landlady from Brighton, finds this recipe goes down well with student guests.

For 8 portions

METRIC	IMPERIAL
100g self-raising flour	**4½oz self-raising flour**
50g cocoa	**1½oz cocoa**
1 × 5ml spoon baking powder	**1 level teaspoon baking powder**
150g soft margarine	**6oz soft margarine**
150g castor sugar	**6oz castor sugar**
3 eggs	**3 eggs**
3 × 15ml spoons milk	**3 tablespoons milk**
CHOCOLATE BUTTER ICING	CHOCOLATE BUTTER ICING
100g plain chocolate	**4oz plain chocolate**
200g icing sugar	**8oz icing sugar**
100g butter	**4oz butter**
Chocolate vermicelli	**Chocolate vermicelli**
9 shelled walnut halves	**9 shelled walnut halves**

1. Prepare a cool oven (170 deg C, 325 deg F, Gas Mark 3). Brush a deep, round 20cm (8in) cake tin with melted fat. Line base with greaseproof paper; grease paper.

2. Sift flour, cocoa and baking powder into a bowl. Add margarine, sugar, eggs and milk. Mix together with a wooden spoon; beat for 1 to 2 minutes, until smooth and glossy. Place mixture in tin and level top.

3. Bake in centre of oven for 55 minutes to 1 hour 10 minutes. Test by pressing with the fingers. If cooked, cake should spring back and have begun to shrink from side of tin. Leave to cool in tin for 5 minutes. Loosen edge with a round-ended knife; turn out cake, remove paper and leave to cool completely on a wire rack.

4. Break up chocolate; place in a small, dry basin over a small saucepan of hot, but not boiling, water. Stir occasionally until chocolate has melted.

5. Sift icing sugar into a bowl. Add butter and beat together with a wooden spoon, until light and fluffy. Gradually beat in melted chocolate. Place one third of butter icing in a nylon piping bag fitted with a medium-sized star tube; reserve for decoration.

6. Cut cake into 3 layers. Sandwich bottom and centre layers together with some of the butter icing from bowl. Spread butter icing around side of cake. Place chocolate vermicelli on a piece of greaseproof paper. Hold top and bottom of cake between the hands and roll in chocolate vermicelli, to coat. Repeat with top layer. Spread some icing on top of double layer and remainder over top.

7. Cut top layer into 8 equal wedges. Mark top of double layer into 8 portions with a large knife. Pipe or spoon 8 swirls of butter icing on each marked line around top edge of the double layer. Arrange wedges on top, each with one side tilted upward against a swirl of butter icing. Pipe a final swirl in centre of cake. Decorate each wedge and centre of gâteau with a walnut half.

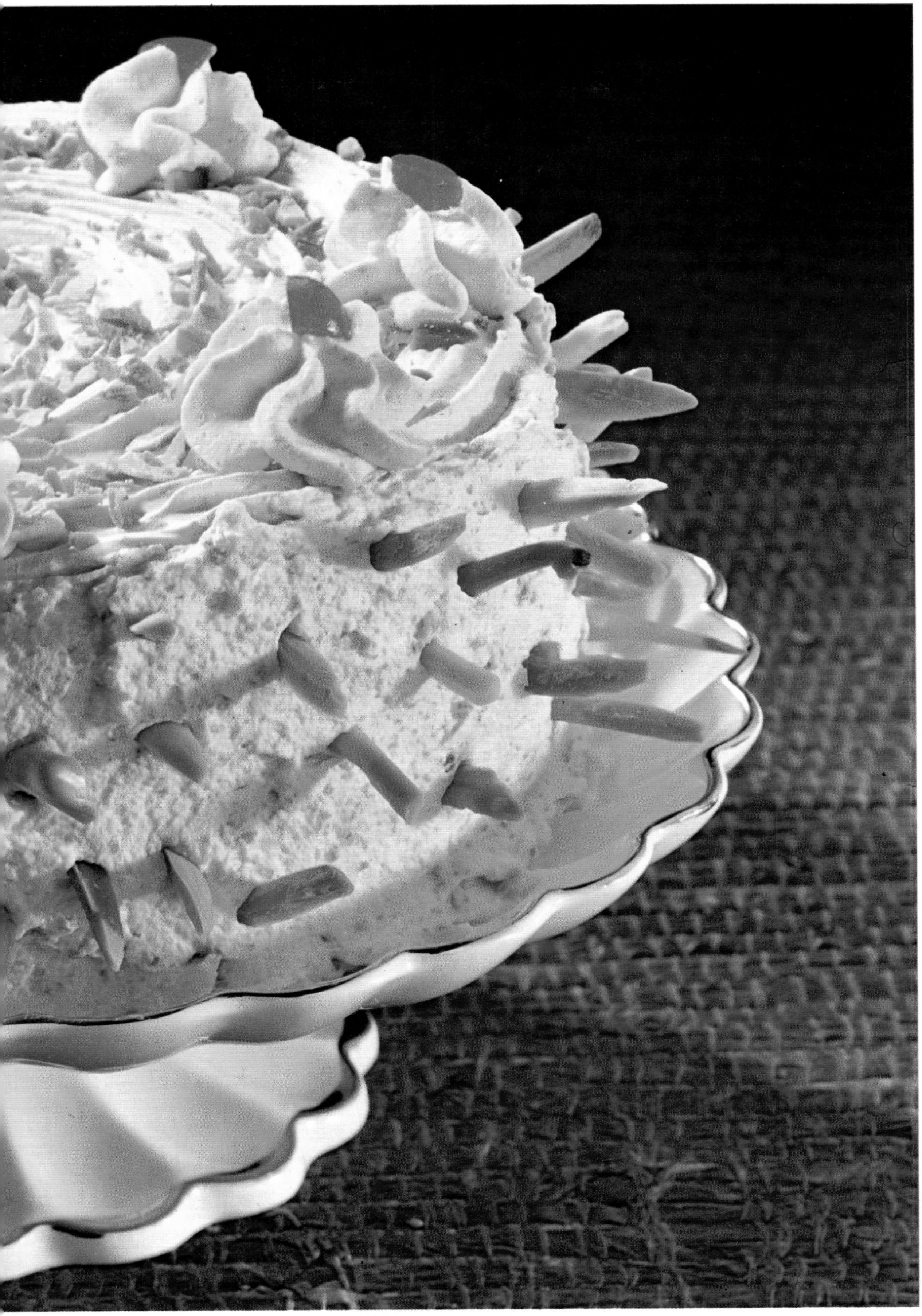

PRALINE AND ALMOND VACHERIN
Recipe on page 86

Praline and Almond Vacherin

(pictured on pages 84/85)

Mrs Gillian Neale, from King's Langley in Hertfordshire, won first prize with this recipe in one of our Cook of the Year competitions.

For 6 portions

METRIC	IMPERIAL
50g shredded almonds	**1½oz shredded almonds**
225g icing sugar	**8½oz icing sugar**
4 egg whites	**4 egg whites**
25g ground almonds	**1oz ground almonds**
3 drops vanilla essence	**3 drops vanilla essence**
PRALINE, FILLING AND DECORATION	**PRALINE, FILLING AND DECORATION**
25g granulated sugar	**1oz granulated sugar**
25g shelled, unblanched almonds	**1oz shelled, unblanched almonds**
300ml double cream	**10 fluid oz double cream**
A few drops vanilla essence	**A few drops vanilla essence**
2 glacé cherries	**2 glacé cherries**

1. Prepare a cool oven (150 deg C, 300 deg F, Gas Mark 2). Place a sheet of silicone-treated paper on each of 2 baking sheets. Draw 2, 15cm or 18cm (6in or 7in) circles on 1 sheet and 1 circle on the other. Half fill a saucepan with water. Bring to boil; remove from heat.
2. Chop 25g (½oz) of the shredded almonds and reserve. Spread remainder on a baking sheet and cook on shelf just above centre of oven for 5 minutes, until lightly browned. Reserve for decoration.
3. Sift icing sugar. Place egg whites in a clean, grease-free bowl. Whisk until foamy; gradually whisk in sugar. Place bowl over saucepan and continue whisking until mixture is thick and leaves a trail when whisk is lifted. Remove bowl from heat and continue whisking until mixture is cool. Fold in ground almonds and vanilla essence. Place mixture in a nylon piping bag, fitted with a large star tube. Pipe mixture inside circles, starting from centre and spiralling out until each circle is filled. Sprinkle reserved chopped almonds over 1 layer of piped meringue.
4. Place 1 baking sheet in centre of oven and 1 just below centre; bake for 30 to 40 minutes, until meringue is dry, crisp and lightly coloured. Leave to cool, then carefully remove from paper; place on a wire rack and leave until completely cold.
5. To make praline: lightly oil a small tin. Place granulated sugar and shelled, unblanched almonds, in a small saucepan. Heat slowly, stirring occasionally, until sugar has melted and turned a caramel colour, and the almonds begin to pop. Pour into oiled tin and leave until cold and set. Crush with a rolling pin to a fine powder, or pulverise in an electric grinder.
6. To make filling: place cream in a bowl; whisk until cream just holds its shape. Carefully fold in a few drops of vanilla essence and 4 × 15ml spoons (2 rounded tablespoons) of the praline powder.
7. To assemble vacherin: place 1 plain circle of meringue on a serving plate; spread with a quarter of praline filling. Top with second plain layer; spread with another quarter of filling. Top with almond-sprinkled layer. Spread half of remaining filling around side and spoon remainder into a piping bag, fitted with a small star tube. Pipe 8 swirls of cream on top of vacherin; top each swirl of cream with a quarter of a glacé cherry. Spike reserved toasted almonds around side.
8. Place vacherin in refrigerator for about 2 hours before serving, as this makes it easier to cut into wedges.

Calypso Creams

(pictured on page 88)

Mrs Kathleen Shultz, from Middlesbrough, Cleveland, was a finalist in a Cook of the Year competition.

For 4 portions

METRIC	IMPERIAL
25g plain chocolate	**1oz plain chocolate**
25g blanched almonds	**1oz blanched almonds**
Green food colouring	**Green food colouring**
1 small (226g) can pineapple rings	**1 small (8oz) can pineapple rings**
2 large lemons	**2 large lemons**
150ml double cream	**5 fluid oz double cream**
1 small can (about 150ml) sweetened condensed milk	**1 small can (about ¼ pint) sweetened condensed milk**
Sponge finger biscuits	**Sponge finger biscuits**

1. Break up chocolate and place on a dry plate over a saucepan of hot, but not boiling, water; stir occasionally, until melted. Spread thinly over a clean, dry marble slab or a cold plate. Leave in a cool place to set, about 10 minutes. Use the tip of a teaspoon to 'curl off' chocolate into small flakes.
2. Finely chop almonds. Place in a screw-topped jar, with 3 drops of green food colouring; shake well until evenly coloured.
3. Drain pineapple; cut each ring into small pieces and divide between 4 small glass dishes.
4. Scrub lemons; finely grate rind on to a plate. Squeeze juice and reserve. Place cream in a large basin; whisk very lightly until cream just holds its shape.
5. Gradually whisk in sweetened condensed milk. Add lemon rind and juice; continue whisking until thick.
6. Quickly pour mixture over pineapple pieces; smooth surface with the back of a spoon.
7. To decorate: gently place a plain cutter, which measures 1cm (½in) less in diameter than the dish, on to cream mixture in 1 dish. Place chocolate curls on cream outside cutter; place nuts inside cutter. Remove cutter, wipe and repeat with remaining creams. Serve creams, chilled, with sponge finger biscuits.

Piquant Meat Loaf

(pictured below)

Mrs Judith Blamey, from Leeds, Yorkshire, won third prize in one of our Cook of the Year competitions with this particular recipe.

For 6 portions

METRIC	IMPERIAL
MEAT LOAF	MEAT LOAF
7 rashers streaky bacon	7 rashers streaky bacon
1 medium-sized onion	1 medium-sized onion
150g minced beef	6oz minced beef
300g pork sausagemeat	¾lb pork sausagemeat
1 × 10ml spoon Worcestershire sauce	2 teaspoons Worcestershire sauce
1 × 10ml spoon chutney	2 level teaspoons chutney
1 × 5ml spoon chopped parsley	1 level teaspoon chopped parsley
50g fresh white breadcrumbs	2oz fresh white breadcrumbs
1 chicken stock cube	1 chicken stock cube
125ml cider	¼ pint cider
1 egg	1 egg
Celery salt	Celery salt
Pepper	Pepper
GLAZE AND GARNISH	GLAZE AND GARNISH
1 chicken stock cube	1 chicken stock cube
1 × 10ml spoon gelatine	1 rounded teaspoon gelatine
8 cucumber slices	8 cucumber slices
Chopped parsley	Chopped parsley
25g canned red pepper	1oz canned red pepper
Shredded lettuce	Shredded lettuce

1. Prepare a moderate oven (190 deg C, 375 deg F, Gas Mark 5).
2. Remove rind and bone from bacon; press rashers flat with a knife. Line base and sides of a 1kg (2lb), 1 litre (2 pint) capacity loaf tin with rashers. Press firmly on to sides of tin.
3. Peel and finely chop onion; place in a bowl, with minced beef, sausagemeat, Worcestershire sauce, chutney, parsley and breadcrumbs. Mix well with a wooden spoon. Crumble in chicken stock cube; stir in cider, egg, a few shakes of celery salt, a shake of pepper.
4. Pour mixture into loaf tin; level top with back of a metal spoon. Cover top of tin with a piece of foil; place tin on a baking sheet.
5. Bake in centre of oven for 40 to 50 minutes, until mixture feels firm.
6. Remove loaf from oven, loosen foil to allow steam to escape and leave loaf in tin until cold.
7. To make glaze: crumble chicken stock cube into a basin; add gelatine and 6 × 15ml spoons (6 tablespoons) water. Place basin in a saucepan of water over a moderate heat; stir until the gelatine and stock cube have dissolved. Remove basin from saucepan; cool.
8. Turn loaf out of tin on to a wire rack over a plate.
9. When glaze has almost set, spoon over meat loaf, to coat evenly. When the glaze has set, place the loaf on a serving dish.
10. Cut 4 cucumber slices in halves; arrange along top edge of loaf down long sides, with cut edges facing inwards. Sprinkle centre with chopped parsley. Drain can of red peppers. Cut red pepper into strips; cut 10 diamond shapes from strips and arrange between each piece of cucumber.
11. Arrange shredded lettuce around loaf on dish and garnish with remaining strips of red pepper and remaining 4 slices of cucumber. Serve cut into slices.

PIQUANT MEAT LOAF

CALYPSO CREAMS *Recipe on page 86*

Golden Chicken Rice Special

Mrs Mary Lea, from Colwyn Bay, was one of the finalists in a Cook of the Year competition.

For 4 portions

METRIC	IMPERIAL
SAVOURY RICE	SAVOURY RICE
1 small onion	1 small onion
75g butter	3oz butter
175g long-grain rice	7oz long-grain rice
1 chicken stock cube	1 chicken stock cube
375ml boiling water	¾ pint boiling water
SAUCE	SAUCE
1 small onion	1 small onion
50g medium-sized mushrooms	2oz medium-sized mushrooms
25g butter	1oz butter
25g cornflour	½oz cornflour
1 chicken stock cube	1 chicken stock cube
125ml dry white wine	4 fluid oz dry white wine
GOLDEN CHICKEN	GOLDEN CHICKEN
Oil for deep frying	Oil for deep frying
2 chicken breasts	2 chicken breasts
2 × 15ml spoons plain flour	2 level tablespoons plain flour
Salt and pepper	Salt and pepper
1 egg, beaten	1 egg, beaten
Fresh white breadcrumbs	Fresh white breadcrumbs
GARNISH	GARNISH
Canned red pepper	Canned red pepper
Sprigs of watercress	Sprigs of watercress

1. Prepare a moderate oven (190 deg C, 375 deg F, Gas Mark 5).
2. To make savoury rice: peel and chop 1 small onion. Melt 50g (1½oz) butter in a frying pan; add onion and fry for 2 to 3 minutes, until onion is soft, but not browned.
3. Add rice and cook for 2 minutes, until rice has absorbed fat. Dissolve stock cube in boiling water. Stir into rice; bring to boil and place in a shallow casserole. Cover with a piece of buttered greaseproof paper and casserole lid. Place in centre of oven and cook for 30 to 35 minutes, until stock is absorbed and rice is cooked. Using fork, stir in remaining butter. Keep warm.
4. To make sauce: peel and chop 1 small onion. Wash and slice mushrooms. Melt 25g (1oz) butter in a frying pan; add chopped onion and mushrooms and fry for 2 to 3 minutes. Measure 250ml (½ pint) water. Blend cornflour with a little of the measured water; stir in remaining water, crumbled stock cube and the wine into frying pan. Bring to boil and cook for 2 minutes.

5. To make golden chicken: fill a deep-fat pan one third full with oil. Heat to 190 deg C (370 deg F) or until a 2.5cm (1in) cube of day-old bread browns in 40 seconds. Remove skin from chicken breasts and cut meat into 1cm (½in) wide strips. Mix flour, a little salt and a shake of pepper together on a plate; turn chicken pieces in seasoned flour, to coat.
6. Place beaten egg on a plate and breadcrumbs on another plate. Coat chicken pieces in beaten egg (allow any excess to drain off), then in breadcrumbs, shaking off excess crumbs. Fry chicken pieces in oil for 5 minutes, until chicken is cooked and golden. Drain on kitchen paper; keep hot.
7. To serve: place rice in a warmed, shallow serving dish. Reheat sauce and pour over the rice. Pile the chicken pieces on top of rice and garnish with strips of red pepper and sprigs of watercress.

Jamaican Delight

Mrs Celia Sandrey, from Guernsey, finds this dessert a top favourite, when she serves it in her guest house.

For 6 portions

METRIC	IMPERIAL
1 (450g) can pineapple pieces	1 (16oz) can pineapple pieces
1 miniature bottle Tia Maria or rum	1 miniature bottle Tia Maria or rum
150ml double cream	5 fluid oz double cream
1 × 10ml spoon castor sugar	1 rounded teaspoon castor sugar
1 × 10ml spoon instant coffee	1 rounded teaspoon instant coffee
1 family-size brick coffee ice cream	1 family-size brick coffee ice cream
6 walnuts	6 walnuts

1. Place pineapple, with a little syrup from can, in 6 glasses. Add 1 × 10ml spoon (2 teaspoons) Tia Maria or rum to pineapple in each glass.
2. Place cream in a basin, add sugar and instant coffee, stir gently until dissolved; whisk until thick.
3. Just before serving, spoon or scoop ice cream into each glass; quickly top each with coffee-flavoured cream and decorate each with a walnut. Serve immediately.

Chocolate Nut Mousse

(pictured below)

Mrs Susan Horton, from Devizes in Wiltshire, was a finalist in one of our Cook of the Year competitions.

For 4 portions

METRIC	IMPERIAL
25g plain chocolate	1oz plain chocolate
2 eggs	2 eggs
1 small (250g) can sweetened chestnut purée	1 small (8¼oz) can sweetened chestnut purée
50g mixed chopped nuts (almonds, hazelnuts, walnuts)	2oz mixed chopped nuts (almonds, hazelnuts, walnuts)
1 × 10ml spoon gelatine	½ level tablespoon gelatine
150ml double cream	5 fluid oz double cream

1. Place chocolate in a dry basin over a small saucepan of hot, but not boiling, water; stir occasionally, until chocolate has melted.

2. Separate eggs; place whites in a clean, grease-free bowl and beat yolks into melted chocolate.

3. Remove from heat; stir in chestnut purée and 25g (1oz) mixed nuts.

4. Place gelatine and 2 × 15ml spoons (2 tablespoons) water in a basin over saucepan of hot water; stir until gelatine has dissolved.

5. Whisk cream until thick. Place 2 × 15ml spoons (1 rounded tablespoon) cream in a nylon piping bag, fitted with a large star tube. Whisk egg whites until stiff, but not dry.

6. Stir gelatine into chocolate mixture. Fold in cream and egg whites, cutting through with a metal spoon.

7. Spoon mixture into 4, 150ml (6 fluid oz) individual serving dishes. Leave to set in refrigerator.

8. Sprinkle the remaining 25g (1oz) mixed nuts on each chocolate mousse and pipe a swirl of cream in centre.

CHOCOLATE NUT MOUSSE

Orange and Peach Flan

Mrs Olive Winzer, from Exmoor, Devon, finds this recipe and the Fruit Salad, right, most popular with her guests.

For 6 portions

METRIC	IMPERIAL
FLAN	FLAN
100g butter	4oz butter
100g castor sugar	4oz castor sugar
2 eggs	2 eggs
Grated rind and juice of half a medium-sized orange	Grated rind and juice of half a medium-sized orange
100g self-raising flour	4oz self-raising flour
FILLING	FILLING
Quarter of an orange-flavour jelly	Quarter of an orange-flavour jelly
Boiling water	Boiling water
1 large (425g) can sliced peaches	1 large (15½oz) can sliced peaches
1 large orange	1 large orange
DECORATION	DECORATION
A little whipped or canned cream	A little whipped or canned cream

1. Prepare a moderate oven (180 deg C, 350 deg F, Gas Mark 4). Brush a 20cm (8in) sponge flan tin generously with melted fat; line base of tin with a circle of greaseproof paper; grease paper.

2. Cream butter and sugar together until light and fluffy. Beat eggs together; add gradually, beating after each addition. Mix in orange rind.

3. Fold in flour alternately with orange juice, cutting through mixture with a metal spoon.

4. Place mixture in tin, level top with spoon and bake in centre of oven for 30 to 40 minutes. Test by pressing with the fingers. If cooked, flan should spring back and have begun to shrink from side of tin. Leave to cool in tin for 10 minutes, then turn out, remove paper and leave to cool completely on a wire rack.

5. Place jelly in a measuring jug and make up to 125ml (¼ pint) with boiling water; stir until jelly has dissolved. Leave in a cool place until just on the point of setting.

6. Drain peaches, reserving syrup, if desired, for Fruit Salad (see right). Using a sharp or serrated knife, cut peel from orange, including white pith. Hold orange over plate to catch juice; cut out segments of orange, discarding pips and pith.

7. Place flan on a plate. Arrange alternate slices of peach and orange, radiating out from centre. (Keep any leftover fruit for Fruit Salad, right).

8. When jelly is cold and on the point of setting, pour over fruit in flan. Leave to set.

9. Place a little whipped cream (or chilled canned cream with whey poured off) in a piping bag, fitted with a star tube; pipe stars around edge. Keep cool until served.

Fruit Salad

For 4 or 5 portions

METRIC	IMPERIAL
2 eating apples	2 eating apples
2 ripe bananas	2 ripe bananas
2 × 15ml spoons lemon juice	2 tablespoons lemon juice
3 × 15ml spoons castor sugar	3 level tablespoons castor sugar
100g grapes	¼lb grapes
2 dessert pears	2 dessert pears
1 large orange	1 large orange
Slices of orange and peach, and peach syrup from Orange and Peach Flan (see left)	Slices of orange and peach, and peach syrup from Orange and Peach Flan (see left)

1. Peel, core and quarter apples; cut across into slices. Peel and slice bananas. Place fruit in a basin, add lemon juice and sugar and mix until fruit is coated with lemon juice. Cover basin with foil and keep in a refrigerator or cold place overnight.

2. Place grapes in a basin, cover with boiling water, leave for 1 minute, then drain and peel off skins. Cut grapes in halves and remove pips. Add to apples and bananas

3. Peel, core and quarter pears. Cut into thin slices and add to other fruit.

4. Using a sharp or serrated knife, cut peel from orange, including white pith. Hold orange over a plate to catch juice; cut out segments of orange. Add orange to basin with reserved fruit and peach syrup (from Orange and Peach Flan, left). Mix well and chill the fruit salad for 2 to 3 hours in the refrigerator before serving.

Chicken and Bacon Kebabs

*Mrs Judith Randall, from Derby, was a finalist in one of
our Cook of the Year competitions.*

For 6 portions

METRIC
MARINADE
75ml oil
**5 × 5ml spoons lemon
  juice**
1 bay leaf
**½ × 2.5ml spoon mixed
  dried herbs**
**1 × 15ml spoon soft
  brown sugar (light)**

KEBABS
2 chicken joints
1 medium-sized onion
Half a green pepper
6 rashers streaky bacon
3 medium-sized tomatoes
6 button mushrooms
**12 pieces canned
  pineapple**
6 bay leaves

SPICY TOMATO
SAUCE
1 medium-sized onion
Half a green pepper
1 clove of garlic
Salt
1 × 15ml spoon oil
**1 × 10ml spoon soft
  brown sugar (light)**
**1 × 15ml spoon lemon
  juice**
**3 × 15ml spoons tomato
  purée**
**1 large (396g) can
  tomatoes**
**4 × 15ml spoons
  pineapple syrup (from
  can)**
Half a chicken stock cube
Pepper

SAVOURY RICE
Half a green pepper
**1 small (198g) can sweet
  corn**
1½ chicken stock cubes
100g long-grain rice

GARNISH
1 lemon
Half a green pepper

IMPERIAL
MARINADE
2½ fluid oz oil
**1½ tablespoons lemon
  juice**
1 bay leaf
**¼ level teaspoon mixed
  dried herbs**
**1 level tablespoon soft
  brown sugar (light)**

KEBABS
2 chicken joints
1 medium-sized onion
Half a green pepper
6 rashers streaky bacon
3 medium-sized tomatoes
6 button mushrooms
**12 pieces canned
  pineapple**
6 bay leaves

SPICY TOMATO
SAUCE
1 medium-sized onion
Half a green pepper
1 clove of garlic
Salt
1 tablespoon oil
**2 level teaspoons soft
  brown sugar (light)**
**1 tablespoon lemon
  juice**
**3 level tablespoons
  tomato purée**
**1 large (14oz) can
  tomatoes**
**4 tablespoons pineapple
  syrup (from
  can)**
Half a chicken stock cube
Pepper

SAVOURY RICE
Half a green pepper
**1 small (7oz) can sweet
  corn**
1½ chicken stock cubes
4oz long-grain rice

GARNISH
1 lemon
Half a green pepper

1. To make marinade: place 75ml (2½ fluid oz) oil and 5 × 5ml spoons (1½ tablespoons) lemon juice in a basin. Crumble or chop bay leaf and add to basin. Stir in herbs and 1 × 15ml spoon (1 level tablespoon) sugar.

2. Remove meat from chicken joints; cut into about 18 small pieces and place in marinade. Peel onion; cut green pepper into bite-sized pieces.

3. Half fill a medium-sized saucepan with water; bring to boil. Add onion and pepper; cook gently for 2 to 3 minutes. Drain and leave to cool.

4. Remove rind and bone from bacon; flatten rashers with a knife. Cut each rasher in half widthwise; roll up each loosely.

5. Cut each tomato into 4 wedges. Wash mushrooms. Cut onion into small pieces.

6. Using 6 skewers, thread pieces of chicken, pepper, onion, bacon rolls, tomato wedges, mushroom, pineapple and bay leaf on to each skewer. Reserve marinade to brush kebabs during cooking.

7. To make spicy tomato sauce: peel and finely chop onion. Chop green pepper finely.

8. Peel clove of garlic; place on a saucer with a little salt. Using a round-ended knife, rub salt against garlic to crush clove.

9. Heat 1 × 15ml spoon (1 tablespoon) oil in a medium-sized saucepan. Add onion, pepper and garlic; fry until onion is tender. Stir in 1 × 10ml spoon (2 level teaspoons) sugar, 1 × 15ml spoon (1 tablespoon) lemon juice, tomato purée, contents of can of tomatoes and pineapple syrup. Crumble in half stock cube; add a little salt and a shake of pepper. Bring to boil, cover and simmer for 20 minutes.

10. To make savoury rice: chop green pepper finely; drain sweet corn.

11. Place 1½ stock cubes and ½ litre (1 pint) water in a medium-sized saucepan. Bring to boil, stir in rice, pepper and sweet corn. Return to boil and cook over a moderate heat for about 12 minutes. Test by pressing a grain between thumb and finger. Drain in a sieve or colander and rinse with hot water. Place rice on a warmed serving dish; keep warm.

12. Meanwhile, prepare a moderate grill. Place kebabs on rack in grill pan; brush generously with marinade. Grill for 10 to 15 minutes, turning occasionally and brushing with marinade.

13. Slice one third off lemon widthwise; place remaining two thirds, cut side downwards, in centre of rice. Arrange kebabs by sticking into lemon at various angles. Cut remaining green pepper into slices and arrange around dish.

14. Pour the spicy tomato sauce into a warmed sauce boat and serve separately with the kebabs.

INDEX

Recipes in alphabetical order

First published in 1978 by FAMILY CIRCLE
1st Reprint 1979
Elm House, Elm Street, London WC1X 0BP. Printed in England by Sackville
Press Billericay Limited, Radford Way, Billericay, Essex CM12 0BZ.
1978 © Standbrook Publications Limited, a member of The Thomson Organisation Limited.
Distributed to the book trade by
Elm Tree Books/Hamish Hamilton Ltd
Garden House 57/59 Long Acre London WC2E 9JZ
ISBN 0 241 10288 X